GROWING HEALTHY THOUGHTS

Claiming Christ Within

MARLENE DOMINY

TATE PUBLISHING
AND ENTERPRISES, LLC

This book is designed to provide accurate and authoritative information with regard to the subject matter covered. This information is given with the understanding that neither the author nor Tate Publishing, LLC is engaged in rendering legal, professional advice. Since the details of your situation are fact dependent, you should additionally seek the services of a competent professional.

The opinions expressed by the author are not necessarily those of Tate Publishing, LLC.

Published by Tate Publishing & Enterprises, LLC
127 E. Trade Center Terrace | Mustang, Oklahoma 73064 USA
1.888.361.9473 | www.tatepublishing.com

Tate Publishing is committed to excellence in the publishing industry. The company reflects the philosophy established by the founders, based on Psalm 68:11,
"The Lord gave the word and great was the company of those who published it."

Book design copyright © 2013 by Tate Publishing, LLC. All rights reserved.
Cover design by Rodrigo Adolfo
Interior design by Mary Jean Archival

Published in the United States of America

ISBN: 978-1-62902-555-1
Self-Help / General
13.10.03

You decide—you either trust God or the
voice of the world around you.

PREFACE

I grew up in Los Angeles during the forties and fifties. Our family was middle class, my father an immigrant from Sweden and my mother a farm girl from Minnesota. Work opportunities brought my father to Los Angeles, a long way from his country home in Sweden. Our family's social and religious life centered on the Swedish church we attended where religious education was fed to me every Sunday.

Life doesn't always work out the way we are told it will, and for me, that was the case. I realized there was a big gap between what I was told as a child in my religious teaching and what I perceived was actually happening. In trying to understand where I had gone wrong and in an attempt to understand life from a bigger perspective, I was led to material that seemed to speak right to my Spirit. When I read and meditated upon truth, I found myself being more at peace and able to accept the circumstance in my life with a new understanding. God really is in control, but too often listening to the nightly news or, sadly, even sitting in a church, we are not given that hope as our grounding for life.

My husband has often said, "If you don't like it, let's see what you can do." I decided it was time to write the book I needed to read. Sometimes we can be just too discouraged to pull ourselves off the ground—we need something that will give us an opportunity to shift our attitude and perspective. I started writing an affirmation each day, thinking that I would write one for each day of the year. Each morning, I tried to fill my mind with positive thoughts that corresponded to the Spirit speaking within me. The thoughts were personalized, and all spoke directly to me. I found they were no longer just ideas to think about but concepts and beliefs I could make a part of my life.

It is so easy to fill our minds with destructive thoughts and negative emotions. I had reached the point where I knew there had to be a better way. For me, it has been the discovery of what God says about me and the circumstances I find myself in and the good news that God truly does have a good plan for me and a good plan for you. Each one of us is an extension of God's love and regardless of what we do and what we think, that can never change. God created us with free will, and that enables each one of us to decide for ourselves how we wish to see our life; false thinking will never make it true, and God has set in place a truth that cannot be changed.

When we focus only on what we do want to have in our lives, we are more likely to reach our goals. *Reading aloud* the affirmations you desire in your life can make a difference. I have learned that choosing what I allow to come into my mind is the first step in changing every other area of my life. We are all blessed with the ability to choose, and making good choices in our thought life is the beginning of making good choices in every other area of life.

Learning should be a joyful experience. It was my intention to present material that would bring joy and hope into my life, and it is my prayer that it will enable you to see a bigger picture of the world we live in and the circumstances that surround you. The power of God is very much working in each one of our lives, and being able to see that on a daily basis can bring a peace that transcends this world. We can truly be in this world but not of this world when we focus on the eternal and not the temporal.

From the day you were born, you were programmed by the people and situations that surrounded you. Each one has played a part in who you are today, but that does not mean you have to live with the regrets and failures of the past. Each day is an opportunity to begin again and rethink how you have been thinking. Each one of us has a special gift of being able to choose our thoughts. Our circumstances may not always be what we want them to be, but we all have a freedom that no one can take away from us, and it resides within each one of us. Treasure your good thoughts, for each one has a value beyond description.

JANUARY

JANUARY 1

What I need to remember today:

I was and am created in the image of God. I am a spiritual being living in a physical body. The seed of God lives within me. God is unlimited, and as such, I am unlimited. I acknowledge his presence and power within me. I claim God's wisdom for my day. My faith closes the door on fear. I will choose faith over fear in all the circumstances I face today. I know God is in control and has a good and loving plan for my life.

JANUARY 2

What I need to affirm today regardless of what happens:

I choose to be a positive person. I know God loves me. There is nothing God cannot make right. I am here for a reason, and God will reveal his purposes to me. I hear God's voice and feel his leading. I am never alone. God dwells within me. I was made for a purpose and God's purposes never fail.

JANUARY 3

I know that:

What I believe and think today will determine my physical future. I am part of a loving, eternal plan created before time. I affirm God's good plan for my life. God is true, eternal, and unchanging, and as such, I can have peace being a part of his eternal and perfect plan. I will see his hand in the situations around me and give thanks for all things. God gives me wisdom to see beyond the circumstances I encounter and to be peaceful regardless of what those around me are doing. I will follow God's leading and not the ways of the world. I am keeping my focus on God and not the world's powers. I am resting in God's provisions for my life and not my own. God knows my needs and provides for them. I am able to discern the hand of God in the people and situations I encounter.

JANUARY 4

I speak health into my life:

I erase all disease from my life. I have health because I claim inner peace. I release all negative thinking and behavior from my body. It is a fit temple for the Holy Spirit. I have been made in the image of God, and I affirm his wholeness as mine. I see and live wholeness in myself and others. My eyes are able to see Christ consciousness in the people and circumstances I encounter. I see all of life as an unfolding of choices of faith or fear, spiritual or physical, ego or spirit. I choose faith, the spiritual and spirit. I empower spirit to lead and direct my life. I rebuke the ego and its lies and give full power to the Spirit that dwells within me. I am Spirit-filled.

JANUARY 5

I will listen to the still, small voice within me:

I put my trust in the Holy Spirit. I accept God's love and provision for me. I choose to hear God's voice today and agree with God and his will for my life. I have decided to see myself within the light of God. I am deprived of nothing of real value. I accept God's gifts to me. I accept the mind of Christ and turn my thought life over to perfect thought. My mind is renewed and refreshed, and I know the truth. I acknowledge the Holy Spirit within me and hear his voice. God speaks to me, and I hear his voice.

JANUARY 6

I have a teachable Spirit and grow wiser each day because:

I seek wisdom and am open to God's teaching. I value God's wisdom and desire to learn. I know who I am in Christ. I am able to discern truth from trash. I am part of Spirit. I choose to see the Spirit in those around me. I know we are all part of one Spirit, one body, and all-important in God's plan. I choose to look beyond ego errors. God will reveal the truth to me so I can share it with those around me. God's thoughts grow as I give them away. I strengthen what I share.

JANUARY 7

I am open to hearing the voice of Spirit and do not fall prey to my ego:

I choose today whose voice I hear. I choose to hear the Holy Spirit and his gentle leading back to God. I see myself as God created me. I choose to erase the errors of the ego. I am as I was designed at the beginning of time. I have a healed mind and hear the voice of truth. I am thankful for the Holy Spirit and his leading in my life.

JANUARY 8

I am a source of light in this world and:

I will bring light to any darkness I encounter. Darkness cannot exist in light. I am light. My Spirit is surrounded by grace, and my true identity is Spirit. I set my mind under the control of the Holy Spirit. I accept faith as a gift from God. I choose faith as my way of seeing. I believe God is greater than any acts of man and that his perfect purpose will succeed. Nothing I can do can alter God's will. I am awakened to truth and my real identity. God's plans cannot fail. I am part of that plan. I see beyond the body to the spiritual and have perfect vision as God's sees. God guarantees his work—I am his work.

JANUARY 9

I am not a slave to my body:

I align my mind with Spirit. I learn from the antics of the body. The body only reflects what I think. I pay attention to what it is telling me and change my thinking. Ego thinking reaps error results. I am responsible for what I think and what I do. I know that God's will is also my will at its deepest level. I ask that God's will be done in my life.

JANUARY 10

What I think today is very important:

I acknowledge that there are no idol thoughts, and I commit my thoughts to the Holy Spirit. I will protect the truth and refrain from attacking the beliefs of others. I will teach in love and not fear. I will not attack the errors in others and will see them through the eyes of Christ. I accept God's forgiveness and am not separated in thought from God. I will not judge others but show mercy as I have received mercy.

JANUARY 11

I relinquish my thoughts to Spirit:

I affirm my worth as God's child. I will see myself and others only in the truth of our true identity. There is no beginning and no ending in Spirit. I am safe and secure in God's love. I align my thinking with God's thoughts, and God's truth is revealed to me. I am honest in my relationships with God and others. I see God's plan at work in all the situations I encounter. I will seek spiritual guidance in the decisions I make today. I accept the power and strength of Christ in my life. I will share what is real in order to increase it and strengthen it.

JANUARY 12

I am a joint heir with Christ:

I call on the seed of Spirit within me to join me in all decisions I make. I accept his strength to lighten my burdens. I will recognize the Holy Spirit in everyone. I will only share those things I want to strengthen. I will hear the voice of the perfect teacher—the Holy Spirit. I will be a good example in sharing what I have learned. I accept my true identity as a child of God and acknowledge it in others.

JANUARY 13

I will notice what I expose myself to today and make good choices:

I will choose my thoughts carefully today. I choose to think with God and reject all lies. I will use my mind for the healing of my body and right thinking. My healed mind reflects wholeness. I see myself as God created me—I am whole and holy.

JANUARY 14

I put up proper boundaries in my life:

I will not accept attack from others. I will not allow others to bring anger into my life. I will focus on God's love and protection and seek his peace and presence in all situations. I will not give into anger and assault. I will remember and acknowledge who I really am. I will teach what I want to learn. I will teach peace in order to have peace.

JANUARY 15

My mind is receptive to the still small voice of God:

I choose today to affirm my connection to God. I am his child and listen for his voice. In every situation, I turn to the Holy Spirit (God's teacher) to show me the way. I am never alone. I accept Christ consciousness through Jesus, and I am awakened to truth. I call on the light of God to dispel all darkness in my life. I am overcoming as Jesus overcame. I walk in his power. I see my body as an instrument of teaching. I learn from the feelings and signals it gives me.

JANUARY 16

Today I recognize that having and being are two different things:

I am motivated to change. I see myself as God sees me. I know I am following the Holy Spirit's leading when I feel joy. I choose to be the mind of God and not just have the mind of God. I am changing my beliefs into my being. God creates only eternal, as such I am eternal. I am not fooled by the ego I created. I am able to discern truth from illusion. I become wiser each day.

JANUARY 17

God creates only the eternal:

I reject all unwholeness in my life. I see myself whole and complete—in perfect health as God created me. I reject all false thoughts about my body. I remember who I am and my creator. I hear the Holy Spirit's voice. I live by truth and not by sight. I am inspired by the Holy Spirit and turn my abilities over to him. I live my life, remembering God's truths. I teach what I believe, and my life reflects my beliefs. The Holy Spirit uses me to heal others. God is consistent—never changing. I count on his results.

JANUARY 18

Today I listen and hear that still, small voice that lives within me:

The Holy Spirit is in my mind and in all minds. I see beyond the temporal to the eternal. I see the Holy Spirit's light in the mind of others. I am used by God to awaken the light within them. I see my brothers and sisters as God sees them—we are all his children. I will help others who have lost their way

JANUARY 19

I make good choices in the thoughts I have today:

I reject fear in my life and affirm God's love. I give up conflict and live in peace. I choose God's kingdom and truth over the ego's lies and fear. I check my attitude and stay on the course God has prepared for me. I will bless all insane behavior around me. I will use it as an opportunity to bless others. I get what I give; I choose to give good things. I will remember that everyone is here by the will of God—all life is his creation.

JANUARY 20

I focus on the eternal:

The ego conflicts are erased in my mind; they have no power over me. My thinking is clear and free from error. God has released his creative power in me. My power increases each day as I more and more accept my true identity. I am God's will, not his wish—what God wills will be done. My will is in alignment with God's will.

JANUARY 21

I remember I am not my ego but a precious child of God created in his image:

I rebuke free will and the choice for the ego. I commend my Spirit and mind into the Holy Spirit's care. I give up my own agenda for the certainly of God's will. The Holy Spirit is my teacher. I will see others as I see myself. I will treat others as I treat myself, and I will think of others as I think of myself. I will learn from my thoughts about others. Light shines away darkness; it doesn't attack it. I am part of the light of God; I dispel darkness in peace.

JANUARY 22

I act on the power within me by remembering that:

I am not separated from God. I have access to the Father, and I accept my oneness with him. God's power is in me, and I accept and recognize God's power within me. My true identity is restored, and I have been released of my false image—the ego. The Holy Spirit is revealing God's will for my life. I choose Spirit over my ego to direct my life. I accept my worthiness as God's creation. God has established my value forever.

JANUARY 23

The perfect teacher (the Holy Spirit) is always with me:

The result of the Holy Spirits teaching is joy. I see and know my united purpose with God. My body and mind are healthy and strong. I see my body as God's instrument. I reject the ego's interpretation that makes me less than whole. I find solutions to body temptations by looking inward. I hear the Holy Spirit's voice in relationship to my desire, and I desire to hear it loud and strong.

JANUARY 24

In every situation today, I know that:

The Holy Spirit gives me the right perspective. I give up all fear for faith. I acknowledge Christ's presence within me and affirm my wholeness in him. My unified mind and purpose gives me health. I have nothing to fear. God is in control.

JANUARY 25

I will not wait for later:

I choose to remember the will of God *now*. I see the root cause of difficulties and am healed. I am not stuck by symptoms but seek the truth and uproot the cause. My thoughts have power, and I use them to correct error. I use nonverbal thoughts to correct the errors in others. I reject insane behavior in others and reject it in myself. I see myself and others as God sees us. I forgive as God forgives. What I give, I get and I choose God's way. God's forgiveness is not restricted; I do not restrict my forgiveness of others.

JANUARY 26

I see the light around me:

My faith is based on God's truth and not the lies of this world. I rebuke fear based on fantasy and secure my life in God's eternal truth. I surround myself with people of light and draw out the light in all situations. I focus on good in order to live good. What I focus on is what I get. I choose to focus on the positive.

JANUARY 27

Today I choose carefully:

I receive only what I am willing to accept. I hear and receive God's voice in my life. I am able to discern truth from lies and use Christ's strength to dismiss the lies of the world. I am strong in the power of Christ. I overcome the world by the power that lives within me. Each day, I become stronger and stronger in my faith and knowledge of my true identity.

JANUARY 28

God is unchanging, and I remember that:

God's view of me and others has never changed. God is unchanging, and I can rely on his provision to complete his plan. There is no flaw in the plan of God. I am part of that plan, and it will succeed. My free will lets me choose when but not if. I am secure in God's perfect plan in eternity. There will be no lost sheep. God's plan includes everyone. It is completely successful. God's eternal plan is without error and birthed in his love for everyone.

JANUARY 29

My worth cannot change:

I am not threatened by the egos of others. I do not need to compete with others to show my worth. I do not attack the insane behavior of others and am able to see behaviors based on the ego for what it is. I acknowledge my true value as God created me, and I am not side-tracked by the false ego-born image in myself and others.

JANUARY 30
Peace will follow me today:

I align my mind with the mind of Christ. I reclaim eternity and know I am an extension of God's will. I choose to remember the truth about myself and dismiss and erase the lies. The Holy Spirit helps me remember who I truly am and gives me the power to have victory over the ego I created. God's peace rests in the spiritual. I choose to live in peace as God intended.

JANUARY 31
Today I remember that:

God is love, and I am an extension of that love. I am healthy and whole as a part of God's love. I accept his love completely and reject any illness that indicates a lesser value. I value myself as God values me, and in him is perfect health. I acknowledge the healing power of Christ in this world and accept it for those around me. I know it is God's will that I be whole and healthy. I am at peace in the altar within where God resides. I accept no other gods in my life.

FEBRUARY

FEBRUARY 1

I will remember today that:

Perfection is of God. I am perfect as God created me; anything else is a false identity based on illusion and error. I ask for knowledge and wisdom to open my mind to truth. Each day, I become more aware of God's truth and peace. I remove all false gods from my life and ask that God's will become my only will.

FEBRUARY 2

The world does not define me:

I affirm God as my creator and focus on the eternal. I am an extension of God and not a projection of the ego. I choose God's image of me and reject my false identity based on the ego. I am becoming closer to God and further from my ego as I turn my thoughts to the eternal truths. I follow the light of Jesus that leads me to the Father. There are no beginnings and endings in God. I am only restored to my eternal identity, and it is the end of separation and time.

FEBRUARY 3

I will have peace today:

I have a place in God's mind forever. I can never outgive God. I ask for God's will in every situation I encounter today. I have true peace because I know that my true will conforms to God's will. The Holy Spirit is in my mind and reminds me of what I have and who I am. I am led by the perfect teacher and counselor. God speaks through the Holy Spirit to me. God's will and my will are the same—that all God's sons be one and united in him.

FEBRUARY 4

I am not separated from God:

I reject the separation of sickness in my life. I claim healing and wholeness in my life. I hear the voice of the Holy Spirit in my life. I reject the lies of the ego and am able to hear the truth. God's comforter (the Holy Spirit) is always with me. I am never alone. I experience God's peace that surrounds me. I choose God's light over the darkness in the world. My goal was set by God before the beginning of time. My goal cannot be lost. I am loving and whole and welcome God's presence within me. I have the eyes of Christ.

FEBRUARY 5

God's light is within me:

I choose the identity God gave me at creation, and I search within for answers to life's problems. Christ is the doorway to the Father, and I accept Christ's love for me and through it know the love of my Father. I reject all fear that brings on sickness. I bring God's light to all fearful situations. All power is of God. I will not allow any fearful situation to separate me from God. I know that God's purpose can and has been accomplished.

FEBRUARY 6

God's plan is whole and complete:

God's purpose has been accomplished. I choose to see myself in a completed state. My errors in time do not diminish my real being. I am becoming more and more in the physical as I already am in the spiritual. I learn daily from the lessons around me. I am used of God to reflect his will in this world. Faith in the unseen allows me to look beyond the physical. I am a part of Christ and, as such, have complete victory over the ego in my life. My ego has been crucified, and I am resurrected with Christ. My life reflects the resurrection and not the crucifixion. What is real can never die. I affirm that I live forever in Spirit. I am able to discover the eternal from the perishable. Loving thoughts are always eternal. I choose the eternal.

FEBRUARY 7

God's creations are eternal:

I choose the eternal over the material things of this world. I value what God created. I can discern the difference from what I made and what I create. I am able to create with God, and what I make has no real, lasting value. I ask for and seek God's wisdom in my life. The Holy Spirit is my teacher and will answer any and all specific questions I have. I accept others as the Father accepts me. God's presence is with me everywhere. What I accept from God, I am able to give to others, and I then receive what I give. I love myself as the Father loves me, and as such, I am a healed person. I reject all toxic thoughts; they are not of God. My mind is aligned with God's mind.

FEBRUARY 8

Truth is revealed to me today:

I exchange all fear in my life for truth. I pray:

Holy Spirit, teach me the truth about myself and others.

I don't respond to the errors in others. I don't try and analyze, interpret, or justify insane behavior in others. Faith allows me to do nothing. I do not make the unreal real for me by investing my thoughts and actions in them.

FEBRUARY 9

I reflect quietly on the situations I encounter today:

I do not judge what I do not understand. I will appreciate those around me. I will replace fear with love. I choose love over fear in every situation. I am quiet in the midst of turmoil. I am able to hear God's voice and see his light. I will accomplish God's purpose for me. I hide nothing from God's healing light. I will not invest in the world's solutions but in the source. I will not try and save my ego by becoming angry. I will only offer peace. I clean up my mind in order to clean up my external circumstances.

FEBRUARY 10

Today I remind myself of who I truly am:

I am guided daily by the Holy Spirit. My true inheritance comes from God. I know there are no disinherited parts of God's family, for God is wholly, and all that he created is whole. I accept my inheritance and see the great value of others. I never try and equalize myself with others through attack. Since I am in Christ, I have his attributes. The Holy Spirit makes me more aware of God's plan for my life daily. The circumstances in my life are lessons leading me back to God. I will learn the lessons to be learned and remember that I am redeemed.

FEBRUARY 11

I remember that everyone is included in God's plan:

I apply the Holy Spirit's teaching to everyone—there are no lost souls, only lost egos. All are one in Christ. Lessons can be graded by their results. I noticed the results in my life and make corrections. I am guiltless in eternity before God and have no need to attack myself or others. I see myself and others as worthy of God's love and accept his evaluation of myself and others. Love does not kill to save. God is love.

FEBRUARY 12

I live with the awareness of my true nature:

I remain as God created me. I am aware of my eternal nature and know it is unchanging. I have awakened to the truth of who I really am and rid myself of guilt and the need for time. I no longer cover my memory of God with fear. I welcome God's love into my life. I lay all my hurt and pain before the Holy Spirit, and I am healed. I am healed completely; there is no darkness within me.

FEBRUARY 13

I value each moment:

Each moment, I remember the eternal. I do not use time to dig in the past. Each second I am born anew. I choose to acknowledge and accept my eternal identity and not the lies of the ego. I use time to heal distorted thinking and seeing. My mind is free of all darkness. God's light shines on me. I see everyone through the eyes of Christ and release them from their past. I am a person who forgives as God forgives. I am not imprisoned by the past, and I do not imprison others. I will enjoy the love in the present moment.

FEBRUARY 14

The light of Christ shines on me and those around me:

I will see Christ's light in others in order to strengthen it in myself. I have been set free. By my free will, I accept my true identity as God's precious child. I no longer forget and reject what God has given me. I no longer deny my true identity as a child of God. I no longer value the ego I made and the world I once valued. I am awakening in Christ.

FEBRUARY 15

I am released from the burdens of the past:

The Holy Spirit heals me from the scars of the past. I live in the *now* and am released from the baggage of my past. The light of this present moment removes all darkness in my life. I focus on the good possibilities and not my circumstances. I can never lose God's gift to me—unconditional love. I am secure in his love for me. What I see in other, I see in myself. I see God's hand and divine plan in those around me. I see others as God sees them. I don't allow relationships to hold me in the past. Each day, I am born again. I am as God created me. The Holy Spirit restores my vision and shows me perfect purity.

FEBRUARY 16

I remind myself today that God's plan does not fail:

The mission of God, Jesus, and the Holy Spirit will succeed. I learn from the challenges in my life. I learn what to do and what not to do by the teaching aids put in my life. God's will, will not fail. God's will is also my will. I am blessed beyond my physical vision. I accept God's complete forgiveness of the false self I have made. I reject the false beliefs of the ego and surrender my thoughts to God. I value only the eternal. Only truth is true and real. All else is nothing and has no value. I am able to see God in the truth around me.

FEBRUARY 17

Today I remember that:

I am released of guilt. I choose the resurrection over the crucifixion. I give out only that which I wish to receive. The Holy Spirit leads me to salvation and the end of guilt. I allow the Holy Spirit to decide for me in every situation. I acknowledge the Holy Spirit within me and think and act through his leading. The Holy Spirit is my teacher who cannot fail. I accept what God has freely given me. I feel his presence and love.

FEBRUARY 18

I listen for and hear the voice of God:

I accept God's forgiveness and his evaluation of who I am. God created me out of himself. I hear the voice of God through the Holy Spirit. I leave all decisions to him. I am led by the Holy Spirit who answers in all situations. I accept God's unconditional love. I focus on what God made and his perfect plan. I focus on the eternal and not the temporal. Only the eternal is real; the temporal will all pass away.

FEBRUARY 19

Today I remember that I am God's instrument of peace:

I will learn from those who need teaching. I live within the circle of God's peace. I am able to attract others to the peace of God. Everyone I meet, I place within the holy circle of at-one-ment. I quietly bring everyone into the holy circle of God's peace. I share God's holiness with those around me in peace.

FEBRUARY 20

I remember the power of love and know that:

Love is always more powerful than attack. I bring love wherever I go. My mind is restored to the truth. The Holy Spirit leads me to correct interpretation. I grow daily in God's knowledge. I apply it to my life. The truth overcomes the fear in my life. I am able to do all that the Holy Spirit asks me to do. I reveal all darkness in my life to the healing light of the Holy Spirit. All darkness in my life has been replaced by the light of God. I know God's will and purpose. My mind is in alignment with the mind of God. The Holy Spirit is my connection to God. He teaches me the lessons I need to learn. I am a good and willing student.

FEBRUARY 21

I am a reflection of God everywhere I go today:

All illusions in my life have been transformed into truth. God's holy place is within me. I acknowledge its presence. I see holiness in everything God created. I am a spotless mirror reflecting God within me. I see others beyond their egos and reveal the wholeness within them. Eternity and guiltlessness reflect God. God's power is in me, and God's power is limitless.

FEBRUARY 22

I am a reflection of God's peace in this world:

I reflect who I am as God created me. I am God's child and see others as children of God. I have been born of Spirit in eternity. God's power flows through me. I have let go of the past. My true will aligns with God's will. I live in God's peace. I relinquish all problems to the Holy Spirit. I am set free from all past errors and live in peace. I am calm and quiet within.

FEBRUARY 23

I cherish each moment because:

Every moment, I exchange hell on earth for heaven on earth. I follow the Holy Spirit leading to the heaven within me. I am secure in God's love. Each instant, I am born anew. Each instant, I choose God. I see myself free from the past and remember God and my changelessness before him. My eyes are open to all faulty beliefs, and I know the truth. The ego in me has no power over me, and I am free through the power of the Holy Spirit.

FEBRUARY 24

I remind myself that:

My body and mind are host to God. My value is based on what God says about me. I am his priceless child and part of his perfect plan. I willingly take the holiness of Christ for myself. My mind is open to hearing God's voice. I have no hidden thoughts. I am a clear source of communication from the Father. I hear his voice. The Holy Spirit has removed all hidden thoughts from my mind. I am a good and willing host to God. I acknowledge his healing presence in my life.

FEBRUARY 25

I am able to see through the eyes of Christ:

I do not judge. I am under the guidance of the Holy Spirit and serve his needs. I see the wholeness of God's plan and am able to see God's love in my life and in those around me. We are all one with Christ, and God shares himself with Christ. I am aware of the perfect love with me—Christ. I strengthen the truths of God by sharing them. My earthly journey is complete in eternity, and only eternity is real. I am connected to the source of complete and perfect love. There is no darkness in me. The Holy Spirit has removed all darkness. I harbor no bitterness and unforgiveness. I surrender all that is not of God to the healing power of the Holy Spirit. I am healed.

FEBRUARY 26

I remember the will of God and know that:

Love brings no guilt. I rebuke all fear as a learning device. My mind is open to truth and I am, and I do share it with others. I freely give the things of this world to God for his will to be done. I am connected to my heavenly Father and lack nothing of real value. God's will cannot be denied. I am joined to God through Christ. God's will is done—its success is certain. My relationship with God is paramount and the only relationship with real meaning. I am able to see others through the eyes of Christ. I am able to see beyond the darkness of the world. God's glory is revealed to me and through me. I am the guiltless child of God. My false self was crucified with Jesus, and my true identity was restored in the resurrection. I am whole and holy before God. God's grace is unlimited, and I am able to see his grace in others. I do not limit God. I am one with the perfect and completed Son of God.

FEBRUARY 27

I am blessed:

All fear has been replaced with love. I am one with Christ. I give up fear for love—God is love. I choose the peace of God. I recognize Christ who lives within me and surrender everything that would and does hurt me to his healing touch. I have peace since I am one in Christ. I use my mind to communicate God's love. I am released from all false thoughts through the power of the Holy Spirit. I remember my true identity and am never alone. I allow the Holy Spirit to interpret everything for me.

Prayer:

Holy Spirit bless and enter all my relationships.

FEBRUARY 28

God's love never fails:

I accept the miracle of God's love. I accept his total plan of holiness and acknowledge and welcome God's presence. I see the truth because I want the truth. I am able to hear God. I am safe and secure in reality. The Holy Spirit has solved every problem I have given him. I am a teacher of peace. I replace suffering with joy. I am aware of the Holy Spirit's presence in my life. God's kingdom is perfect and eternal.

MARCH

MARCH 1

My free will is a gift from God, and I use it wisely:

By my free will, I accept the awareness of my identity in Christ. I live in Christ's identity and have overcome the world. My mind is set free from illusion, and I am truth. I live in the strength of God that dwells within me. I am whole and holy. I remove all barriers to love. I replace all bitterness and unforgiveness with love. I surrender completely to my true identity in Christ and am no longer blinded by the world. My vision is clear in Christ.

MARCH 2

I remember God's truth and know:

There is no hate in me. I am as God created me. The love of God is in me, and I am safe and secure forever. I accept God's fullness in my life—I lack nothing. I am complete in God. I choose God's truth over the illusion of the world. God is able to use me to reveal his truth.

Prayer:

> Holy Spirit, I relinquish all of life's challenges to you and ask to see everything and everybody through your perspective.

MARCH 3

I accept this present moment as a gift from God:

I live in the present. I invite the Holy Spirit to reveal himself in all the *now* moments of my life. I am filled with his peace, truth, and perfect gentleness. I receive what God has given. I am part of God's will, and it is complete. True vision is restored to me. All false illusions are forgiven. I accept my true identity and relationship to God. I am aware of my holiness in Christ. I accept all forgiveness and love and ask that God's will be done on earth as it is in heaven.

MARCH 4

I open my hands, heart, and mind:

I withhold nothing from God. I release everything and everybody to the will of God. I hold nothing back. I see the truth in all situations and in those around me. I can and do look beyond the illusions of this world to the truth of God. I have forgiven myself and others—there is no unforgiveness in me. I look beyond and erase the errors of others. I see others in the *now* moment. I do not live in the past. My vision has been restored to the truth of God. I have awakened to God's perfect plan. I am at peace.

MARCH 5
Vision is restored to me:

All guilt has been removed from my life. I have been rebooted through Christ as God intended me to be. I am filled with loving thoughts. I see the spark of God in everyone around me. The Holy Spirit teaches me from my past and then allows me to release it. There is no dis-ease in me. I value only the eternal; all else is illusion. I bring joy to those around me. I live in the joy of God. I remember and restore the relationship I have with the Holy Spirit. I have spiritual vision and look beyond the physical. I have the power of heaven in me. I am able, through the love of God, tears of Christ, and joy of the Holy Spirit, to defend all attacks I incur. I surrender all unholy relationships to the Holy Spirit to use as he pleases.

MARCH 6
My goal of seeking God is clear:

I have decided in advance what my goal is, and it is God's will as well. Truth and sanity are my goals. I know God's plan is whole and complete, and I am part of God's plan. My faith grows daily. God gives me what I need and ask for. I ask for more faith and wisdom. Each day, my faith and wisdom grows. My faith allows me to see the truth in myself and others. I see God's loving hand in everything. My past is forgiven and erased. It has no hold on me today or in the days to come. I accept the Holy Spirit's purpose in all my relationships.

MARCH 7

Peace surrounds me:

I am a giver of peace because I know the truth through faith. I am one with Christ. The Holy Spirit has restored my vision of oneness. I am free of fear and filled with faith. God's truth overcomes all errors. I live in God's truth. I have been restored. The sanity of God is within me. I rest in the quiet center of my soul. I am at peace.

MARCH 8

Today I remember who lives within me:

I live in the reality of God's love. My will is one with God. I see the speck of God in everyone. I am as God created me. I give up all false illusions and am restored. I am the dwelling place of God. I am worthy of his presence. God's will is unlimited and will be done. God created me for his presence. I am worthy. I relinquish all my plans for God's plan; it is complete and whole. I release myself to God and hear his voice.

MARCH 9

I am free from guilt, fear, suffering, and death:

All fear and hatred are gone from my life. I have been forgiven. I am part of God's purpose. I offer all relationships to the Holy Spirit for his purposes. God has revealed the kingdom of heaven within me. All my guilt has been removed. I am free from the fear of suffering and death. I am surrounded by God; my body is not my protection. I am not limited to my body. I perceive my body properly and know it can never contain me. God created the eternal, and I am part of the eternal. I am able to see myself beyond the body and know I am eternal.

MARCH 10
A beautiful day waits before me:

I give up all pain and destruction for the atonement (at-one-ment). Being totally in the present restores my vision. I submit totally to the *now* as God created it. I am aware of the Holy Spirit's presence and am directed by his leading. God's love is unlimited. I am part of that love as an extension of God, and I am made in his image. I am part of the whole. I no longer see myself separate and alone. God dwells within me. I have been awakened to the truth of who I am. I am the source of God's truth in this world. I reflect God's presence and truth in my daily walk. My life reflects living water and quiet gardens leading to the kingdom of heaven.

MARCH 11
I am as God created me:

All errors of the body have been corrected in me. My vision has been restored, and I am free of fear and guilt. My innocence has been restored and covered by purity and love. I am healed though complete forgiveness. I dedicate all situations to the truth of God. Peace is restored in my life. I experience God's healing in my life.

I am part of the wholeness of God. I am not lacking and claim my wholeness.

MARCH 12

I am constantly moving toward God's perfect plan:

There is nothing faith cannot forgive. All my errors have been corrected. I learn from errors and move forward in freedom. I am an immortal creation of God. There is no opposite. God cannot be corrupted. His plan is certain and complete. There is no power beyond the power of God. I am secure in God's love, power, and plan. My mind is healed of all false thinking, and I recognize the truth. I have been resurrected with Jesus and am restored and redeemed. I remember my relationship with God and all his children. I know who I am as God's child.

MARCH 13

God's security surrounds me:

I am completely protected by God's plan. I am surrounded by love, safety, and freedom. I submit to the Holy Spirit's function on earth. I desire peace and give up all barriers of separation and attack. I remove anything that keeps me from a holy relationship with God and all his sons. I am able to see absolute truth. I rest in God's love. I accept Jesus's gift of the resurrection. I see myself as a resurrected body. My salvation is secure in the eternal and beyond the body. I accept the power of Jesus in my life and have overcome the world. I have faith in the eternal and am kind, patient, and loving.

MARCH 14

Health and serenity surround me:

I send loving messages to my body. It is full of health and reflects God's power within me. God has forgiven and released me from all my burdens. I am at one with the will of God. Salvation is guarded by God's love and will never change. I surrender all my fears to the holy one that lives within me. God has restored my will to his will, and all obstacles have been removed. I am free from the past and live in the precious present. I accept complete forgiveness for myself. I give forgiveness to others. I receive what I give. I see myself and others through the eyes of Christ.

MARCH 15

I represent the Christ that lives within me:

I know and accept only truth—the sure protection and perfect plan of the Father. I am one with the risen Christ and am forgiven, healed, and whole. My innocence lies in Christ. The Holy Spirit has given me his vision. The holiness within me leads me home. I am reawakened to the laws of God and rest in his love and protection. I see Christ in everyone I meet. I see them as God created them—sinless children of God. I offer forgiveness in every situation. God's plan is certain, and I am part of God's plan.

MARCH 16

Truth and vision are restored to me:

I know nothing real is ever lost forever. I give up all judgment for the vision of Christ. I am able to see beyond the body and its actions to the Holy spark within. I remember God's laws and am at peace. I rest in the Father's gentle hands in safety and in peace. I accept my real relationship with the Father and know wholeness. It is based on love and has no hidden part. My desire is to know and live the truth. I ask to know the truth and have true vision restored. I accept what the Holy Spirit freely gives.

MARCH 17

Peace surrounds me:

I see others as God sees them. I learn from the realities I create, and my true vision is restored. I live in peace and confidence. My mind is stayed on God. I am aligned with God's purposes. I learn life's lessons joyfully and remember truth. My eyes are open to the reality of God, and I remember his holy light that shines on me. I was created by a loving Father. I am led by the Holy Spirit, and I hear his voice.

Prayer:

> Holy Spirit, decide for me. I freely give up my will for God's will.

MARCH 18
I walk in light:

I desire no purpose but God's. I align my mind with the mind of Christ. My faith is secure in the holy. My belief, faith, and vision are based on God's holy plan. I completely accept the goal of God. My faith and belief are restored to truth, and I have true vision. I am not deceived. I am not limited to physical vision. Spiritual vision is restored to me. I am free in the holiness of Christ. I am able to see Christ's holiness in others. I reject all false beliefs about myself and others. I am secure in God's loving plan. I am used of God to enable the blind to see. My spiritual vision brings light to darkness. The Holy Spirit reveals and corrects the errors of my physical experience. I look within and see the light of Christ.

MARCH 19
I am led by the Holy Spirit:

I look for and see holiness. My mind is directed by the Holy Spirit. I see as Christ sees and hear his voice. I am aware of God's reality. My faith rests in truth. My worth in beyond measure and is established for eternity. What God wills will be done. I rest in God's will; it is certain to succeed. The power that is within me corrects all errors. I accept what God intends me to give to others. I see myself only through the loving eyes of Christ. I remove all false barriers to true vision. I extend healing to all I meet. I see Christ's wholeness in myself and everyone I meet. I am able to teach the truth through the power of the Holy Spirit in me.

MARCH 20

I am part of God's perfect plan:

The power within me is greater than any of my errors. I give what I accept for myself. I accept Christ's power within me and complete forgiveness. I extend healing to everyone I meet. I see Christ's wholeness in me and in others. I am taught daily by the Holy Spirit. God's eternal plan is based on love. I am part of that plan, and it will not fail. I am able to see the world through the eyes of Christ and know his purposes will succeed. My life is one of truth, power, and healing. All my thoughts are dedicated to God. I remove and willingly give up everything that keeps me from my awareness of God.

MARCH 21

I focus and remember the truth that never changes and know that:

I am complete as God made me. My will is God's will. I am one in Christ. I am a part of God's holy relationship with his children. I am worthy. I remember the truth and am joyful. The truth never changes, and I am secure in the truth of God. I have been released of all guilt and extend this same release to everyone. I look beyond the errors in others and see their eternal future. I enable others to see their destiny as God created them. I have pure thoughts toward myself and others.

MARCH 22
I am part of God's saving plan, and I know:

All false illusions have been replaced by knowledge and truth. I grow daily in God's wisdom and share it with those in darkness. I am a light in this world and give hope and comfort. I see beyond errors to holiness. My spiritual eyes are stronger than my physical eyes. I do not attack the insane behavior of others. I forgive them their errors. I forgive as Christ forgave. I feel God's strong hand guiding and protecting me. I have nothing to fear.

MARCH 23
In all situations, I remember who established my value:

I love all that God loves and in the eternal God loves all. I remember the limitless and eternal and know I am the will of God. My value is secure and certain and will never change. I am a child of God and designed for his purpose. I do not attack God's children. I know we are all part of the body of Christ—we are all one. My value is established by God, and nothing can change that. I do not allow others to establish my value. I am secure in God's plan.

MARCH 24
I reflect love and peace:

I am God's light of love in this world. I see through the eyes of Christ. My spiritual memory has been restored. God loves me perfectly, completely, and eternally. I am a part of that love. I am able to see truth and live in its assurance. There is no conflict in me, and I am at peace. There is nothing I will not forgive. I know God's peace in forgiveness and pass peace on to those around me.

MARCH 25

Truth does not change:

Truth is the same for everyone. All errors disappear when brought to the light of truth. I am secure in God's unchanging plan. My mind is at peace. My life is secure in heaven where God created life. My choices reveal heaven to me. I feel God's guiding hand bringing heaven into my life. I give what I want to receive—love and forgiveness. I do not attack myself or others. I am an instrument of peace.

MARCH 26

God has but one purpose:

My purpose is part of God's purpose. I willingly accept God's purpose for my life. I am a part of the body of Christ, and his power is within me. I accept God's peace as it is his will for me. I have no enemies and am at peace. I am an extension of God's love. I am equal in eternity. I no longer condemn myself and freely receive God's love. I rest secure in God's love and know peace. I am awaken to the eternal life within me and know myself as God created me. I forgive all false illusions about myself and others. As I give, I receive. I am God's child, resting in him. I have awakened to my birthright.

MARCH 27

The power of Christ is within me:

I have no enemies, and I choose not to attack. I see God's holiness in others and choose to heal instead of hurt. I do not cast stones that come back to hit me. I am a part of God's love and peace, and it is returned to me. I am still and know the Christ that lives within me. I forgive as Christ forgave and know the truth of Christ. Christ's hand hold's all his brothers to himself. My journey is secure in him. I am one with Christ and am complete. All doubt has been exchanged for certainly. My life is lived through Christ.

MARCH 28

I am complete and whole:

I am a part of God's plan. I am an extension of eternal thought and have great value. I am a part of the whole that makes God's plan complete. God's plan is complete and has no missing parts. The truth of eternity is unchanging. I see myself and all others as part of God's perfect plan. I look beyond error to holiness. Christ in me sees the Christ in others. I am connected to my heavenly Father through Christ. I recognize Christ in me and everyone. God's will is done.

MARCH 29

In spite of what happens, I defer to my true identity and know that:

I am safe as God created me. I am God's beloved child. I remember who I am. I live secure in God's eternal plan and see that plan in everyone. I choose God's identity of myself over the identity of this world. The holiness of Christ dwells within me. I look beyond bodies to the Christ that dwells within. I accept and acknowledge Christ's presence within me. My mind is healed of all false thinking.

MARCH 30

The light of Christ shines through me:

The power of Christ is in me. I can do all that God appoints me to do. I am united with Christ. My body is the holy frame that holds Christ's holiness. I see others as I see myself. God's light has removed all darkness in my life. My mind is clear to truth, and I experience God's peace. I am following the Holy Spirit's leading. I reveal Christ to the world and see in them what they are unwilling to see. My beliefs are based in truth and not perception. I call on heaven's help to reinterpret God's way. I choose love over anger and peace over war. I see through God's eyes.

MARCH 31

God's plan is complete and perfect, and I know that:

God is the bookends of my existence. I am created for eternity. I relinquish the desires of the ego and the need for time for truth. I see and reflect the world that God created. I bring God's light and truth to darkness. I constantly choose God's view and not the worlds. I offer peace to everyone. God's will is reflected though me. Truth is and has been restored, and all my mistakes, errors, and illusions have disappeared in the light of God's truth. I no longer attack, and I no longer live in guilt. My sinlessness is secure in Christ, and he lives within me. God's power of love is beyond all hatred. God's power to save is beyond all egos. God's will, will be done.

APRIL

APRIL 1

I feel God's will surrounding me:

I am healed and blessed by the grace of God. I am no longer blinded by the darkness of the world but see God's light in every circumstance. I know God has a function for everyone in the world. I am completing and fulfilling my function. I forgive, and sin is transformed into salvation. My peace comes from the will of God. I accept God's blessings. I am part of his will. I give up all illusions, wishes, and dreams for the will of God. I rest secure in God's love.

APRIL 2

I hear and know the voice of truth:

The Holy Spirit is my teacher. I willingly submit to his teaching and hear his voice. There is nothing I hold back from change, and I am able to understand and accept truth. I see my worth as God sees it. I am an extension of his love and exist for his purpose. My will and God's will are the same. I give up my illusions of time and the ego for God's truth and eternity. I look past the temporal and physical and see God. God created everyone equally, and we all exist as part of the body of Christ. God has no lost sheep. There is perfect justice and perfect peace in God's plan.

APRIL 3

I am a vessel of peace in this world:

I live in the grace of God and fully accept his gift of salvation. I give what I have received. The Holy Spirit corrects all problems with complete justice. I accept God's gifts of healing, deliverance, and peace. I surrender all my problems and faulty thinking to the Holy Spirit. I pass on the pardon and forgiveness I have accepted and received to others. I am accepted by God and live in his love and grace. My mind is at peace.

APRIL 4

I am whole in Christ:

I am able to see spiritual truth in every situation. I am fulfilling the special function God gave me. I am part of God's perfect will. I rest secure in the love of God. His eternal plan never changes. I am part of that plan and surrender the free will that has led me to false illusions. I choose heaven over hell in every situation. I am one in Christ and no longer see myself as separate. God is the creator of one creation, one reality, and one son. My faith rests on truth and not illusion. God's truth is revealed to me daily, and I walk secure in that truth. I am part of

God's total forgiveness as are all those that walk around me. I am able to see the unity in Christ.

APRIL 5

I live a resurrected life:

I am one with the sinless one—Christ who lives within me. I give up my false identity for the sinless. Heaven is revealed to me. I always choose God's teacher to lead me home. I have the eyes of Christ. I see as Jesus saw and live with eternal vision. I accept Christ's gift of the resurrection. I have died to self (my ego) and am resurrected in Christ. I no longer live in the past but the present, no longer in fear but in faith, and no longer in darkness but light. I accept total forgiveness for the past I created and reclaim my identity in Christ. I extend this forgiveness to others. God has no lost sheep.

APRIL 6

Peace surrounds me:

I accept God's will for my life. The power and purity of Christ lives through me. Sickness has no power in my life. I am free of sin and its consequences. I reject all false belief and live a life of truth. I have accepted complete forgiveness and live in God's complete love. I am part of God's perfect and complete plan, and God's will is my will. I remember my first and true identity as God created me. I offer forgiveness as the answer to any attack and offer love for hate. I am free from the past and free from the fear of the future. I experience God's peace and love right now. What I accept for myself, I freely give to others. I have released all hatred for love. My soul is at peace.

APRIL 7

I claim God's healing power:

I am aware of the holiness that lives within me. I accept it for myself and see it in others. I reject all guilt in my life and experience health. There is no sickness in me. My body is whole, and the holy dwelling place of Christ in me. The purpose of my body is to serve God. My mind is healed of all error. I forgive and am forgiven. I love and am loved. My mind is no longer split, and I see God's unity. I am able to hear God's voice. I am healed and offer healing to others. All fear has left me. I apply what the Holy Spirit has taught me. I live daily in the healing power of God.

APRIL 8

I am healed by the light of truth:

I have eternal life, and I am at peace. I have awakened to truth and am not afraid. I see myself and others through the eyes of Christ. I am not a victim of someone or something; I do not attack myself or others. My knowledge of eternal life gives me peace. Time cannot intrude upon eternity. My life is lived with eternal vision. I am and always have been secure in God's eternal plan. I am released of all guilt and do not attack myself. All my false illusions are brought to the healing light of truth. I am healed and whole. I walk in wellness.

APRIL 9
God takes center stage in my life:

I allow nothing to take the place of God. I live in the
now and am not bound by the past or future. I trust God
for all the *now* moments in my life and choose the will of
God each moment. My mind is quiet, and my memory of
God is restored. All fear of God has been removed and
erased forever. I rest in God's will that can never fail. I am
a forgiven person and offer that forgiveness to everyone.
I live in peace and happiness. My body is healthy, and I
make good choices in mind and body to keep it well. I
radiate health and good habits.

APRIL 10
God's gifts to us are forever, and I know:

I am united in the body of Christ and am whole in his
healing power. I accept the atonement (at-one-ment) for
myself and others. I see others as God created them, and
I am not put off by error and illusion. I speak God's truth
into every situation. I bring hope and joy to the world. I
see light where others see darkness, and I am a constant
source of light. I always remember who I am as God
created me, and I also am used to help others remember.
God's holiness, complete and perfect, lives in every child
of God waiting to be remembered and recognized. I know
that what God gives cannot be lost. I have the miracle of
the Holy Spirit's sight for myself and others.

APRIL 11

I accept my true identity as God created me:

There is no evil in me, and I am filled with health. I exist because I am a creation of God's will. I am not the illusion I made but the perfect child of God. I am as God created me. I am a forgiving person. I am able to forgive everyone as Christ forgave. I live in his power to forgive. My body is a reflection of my thoughts, and I keep it healthy with good and loving thoughts. I use my body to extend God's will on earth. There is no sickness in me. God's Spirit lives within me, and his Spirit never fails.

APRIL 12

I am a reflection of God's love:

Complete faith has been restored in me. I trust completely in God and am at peace. My body has no power over me. My right thinking gives me health and wholeness. God is always present in my life. I am never in a place God is absent—I live in his will and power. I know God is love. I am able to share his love with others. I reflect God's love and peace and reject all fear and hatred. I accept only what God has given, and I increase it by giving it to others. All life comes from God, and nothing else exists.

APRIL 13

Peace is my constant companion:

I have remembered who I am in Christ. I give what God has given me—total forgiveness. The gift of freedom in Christ has been restored to me. I have no anger toward myself or others. The Holy Spirit reveals true meaning to my dreams of life. God's wisdom is revealed to me, and I am able to see through the changelessness of heaven and the sacred Son of God present within everyone. I am part of a changeless and eternal plan. I am at peace.

APRIL 14

I accept the Holy Spirit's interpretation of events in my life:

I hear God's voice and see his function in others and in the circumstances I encounter. I am able to see through to my eternal identity. I extend total forgiveness in all circumstances and see everyone through the worth God has placed on them. In releasing others, I have released myself from the bondage of the ego (my false self.) All my earthly dreams are given to the Holy Spirit for his use and interpretation.

APRIL 15

God's purpose for my life remains intact:

Through forgiveness, I find peace. My function was fixed by God in eternity, and only the eternal exists. Forgiveness erases all that never was. My eternal purpose is not changed by time—just delayed. When complete forgiveness occurs, time is unnecessary. I practice complete forgiveness daily toward myself and everyone. My forgiveness is as complete as Christ's. I know the truth about myself and others. I am able to look beyond the physical to the eternal within. I lack nothing and am complete in Christ.

APRIL 16

God is my provider:

My soul is God's altar. I give up all idols for truth. I allow nothing to veil the face of Christ. I am able to see God in everything and everyone. God has provided all I need. I no longer judge since I no longer have need of idols. I am released from fear as idols no longer hold my security. My forgiveness has released me from fear.

APRIL 17

I am never alone:

My life is lived in Christ. All my decisions are made jointly with Christ. In every situation, I agree with Christ and not the Antichrist. I hear the Holy Spirit's voice, and God's will is my will. I am complete in God. What God wills is, and I am secure in the changeless character of God. I am complete and whole as God created me, and only what God created is eternal. God's thought of me rests in certainty and peace. False idols no longer block my vision. I see as God sees and know perfect peace.

APRIL 18

I accept my true identity:

I give up the idols in my life. I am free from faith in idols and what I believed they gave me. My complete trust is in God. I forgive as Christ forgave, and I remember the Father. I am complete in the love of the Father. I do not justify anger and see every attack as an opportunity to pardon and forgive. What I give to others, I accept for myself. I accept total pardon and forgiveness for myself and give it to others. I am healthy in body, mind, and spirit. I am part of God's perfect son, and in his glory, I see my own. Nothing can overcome the will of God. I am part of that will and created for God's glory. I have purpose and know peace.

APRIL 19

Only God's plan will succeed:

God's meaning is all there is. I am able to see God's meaning behind all the events in my life. I give up all fear, for all things have but one purpose and one goal. I look beyond appearance to the reality of the changeless. I accept my connection to reality and eliminate the unreal. There is no false doubt and fear in me. I am an instrument for God's miracles in this world. I accept the perfect Christ within me. Daily, I become more aware of the Christ within.

APRIL 20

I am able to hear the still, small voice of the Holy Spirit within me:

I accept truth totally and reject all that is false. I remember God and hear the voice of the Holy Spirit. I see God's son as God created him. I exchange my dreams of illusions for the truth of reality. I know God is love and rest on that assurance. I always choose God's truth over the lies of this world. I am led by the light and companionship of the Holy Spirit. God's peace is within me.

APRIL 21

I remember that I walk among stainless souls:

There is no anger in me. I have been released of all false beliefs. I have given up all belief in sin for total salvation. My mind is healed of all faulty thinking, and I see through the eyes of Christ in me. I have given up all false concepts I have of myself and others. I am not a victim of the world and my circumstances. I offer forgiveness and not blame. I have given up my belief in the flesh for the Spirit. My spiritual eyes grow stronger daily. I see beyond blemished bodies to stainless souls. I choose God's identity of myself and others. I know I am part of God's will, and that can never change.

APRIL 22

I share the truth with those around me:

I always focus on the good in everyone. I look beyond the physical body to the spiritual. I am released of all guilty thoughts and concepts of fear. The Holy Spirit leads me to peace. I look on all with love; there is no hate in me. The present is fresh and clean. I see everything in the *now*. My strength, vision, and identity come from Christ. I learn the lessons of life and teach others. All misery from life's lessons has been changed to joy as the lessons have been learned. In every situation, I choose Christ's strength instead of my own and join in the will of God. I invite God's strength to prevail. I see God in every living thing. All life is his creation. I am able to see God's life force all around me. I am able to feel God's life force within me. I share the truth, and it is strengthened. My purpose is one with Christ, and it will not fail. The roads I have wandered on roll up and disappear when my earthy journey is complete. I have exchanged free will for eternal freedom.

APRIL 23

I choose God's plan over my own:

I know that God's plan is perfection. I choose to be part of God's plan and not my ego-directed plan. I know I am guiltless through Christ and accept my salvation. My words are honest and reflect what I think and do. My thoughts and actions are consistent and reflect God's truth. I do not judge. My life is one of gentleness, and I am released of all dishonest thoughts. I am patient. I know God's outcome and have peace. I know God will make all things right. I have faith in God's love and eternal plan that includes all. It is certain and brings me joy. It is unchanging, and I am tolerant. Christ's forgiveness covers everyone.

APRIL 24

I accept the gift of healing:

Pain has no value in my life. I am strong and whole in Christ. I accept forgiveness for every painful choice I have made and no longer value the pain that sickness brings. My mind is free of thoughts of sickness, and my thinking flows through the mind of Christ. I remember God and my true identity. I am as God created me. I am a part of God's will, and that will never change. I accept God's gift of healing. God's gifts can never run out. He desires to give what I am willing to accept. I accept his good gifts.

APRIL 25

Illusion is replaced by truth:

I give God's gifts to others. I trust in God's eternal outcome. I remember the source of all creation. Truth heals, and I see beyond illusion to the truth beyond. I offer God's healing power over sickness. God's truth restores right thinking. I am surrounded and filled with the truth of God. I accept where and what I am as part of God's plan. There are no accidents in the plan of God, and I am able to see beyond the physical vision that rules this world.

APRIL 26

Wisdom surrounds me because:

I ask for and seek God's wisdom. I rely on the Holy Spirit's interpretation of all situations. I do not judge. I see this world though the word of God and not judgments. I have peace in God's promise of salvation and love. The Holy Spirit is the answer to all problems I made. I turn all my problems over to the Holy Spirit and trust his leading. I hear the voice of Spirit and am led by his teachings. My body is an instrument God uses in this world. He speaks through me to those who need to hear. My health rests in its holy use.

APRIL 27

I am one with Christ:

God is with me. Every decision I make allows me to put my trust in God. I trust God and not the illusions of this world. I am not fooled by the false. Only God's will succeeds. God has not forgotten me, and his love covers all my fears. I am secure in the fact of God and not the fiction of the world. I accept the atonement (at-one-ment) with Christ and know I am God's child. I am aware of my wholeness in God, and true vision is restored.

APRIL 28

Truth is revealed to me:

I offer and accept total forgiveness. I choose the peace of God over all conflict. What God created is eternal, and nothing he did not create is real. His will is without an opposite, and nothing that contradicts his will is true. I am able to see truth from illusion and know the will of God is all there is. In peace, I remember God.

APRIL 29

My life reflects Christ within me:

My words are choosen by God. I hear God's voice in the silence of my heart. I am able to listen, hear, and speak God's words in this world. I am one with Christ. My healing is complete, and I accept complete atonement (at-one-ment). I accept and give total forgiveness and am healed. I see everyone through the eyes of Christ. I do not confuse the body identity and its errors and mistakes with God's creation. I am able to look beyond the miscreations of mankind. The power of God is in me through Christ. I am free of the past and accept at-one-ment *now*. I accept the heaven that is *now* and joyfully accept God's love in my life. I am filled with peace.

APRIL 30

I accept my resurrected life:

I accept my true identity. All barriers to truth have been removed in my life. Death and fear have no power over me. I rest in God's total love. I am the eternal handiwork of God. God has no opposites. I am as God created me and I remember truth. I am not my body but the resurrected child of God. Death has no power over me. I am able to see the joy of heaven on earth. My spiritual vision is strong, and all mistakes are undone. All that remains is truth, and God's children are free from all false illusions. I accept Christ's identity completely, and total freedom is mine. I live the resurrected life and live in the love of God.

MAY

MAY 1

I am able to see and hear the truth:

My Spirit hears the Holy Spirit. True perception has been restored to me, and I remember God. I only see myself through the reflected face of Christ and know the truth. I rest secure in the will of God and know that God's will is all there is. God has no opposites. I see God's forgiven world that looks beyond bodies. True perception has been restored in me, and all illusions are placed on the altar of false belief.

MAY 2

I forgive as God forgives:

There is nothing I will not forgive. I have replaced illusions with holiness, time with eternity, and fear with love. I no longer accept the false but live in God's truth. I am able to discern the true from the false. I accept the resurrected power of Jesus and follow his example. I am a part of the perfect son of God. I join my will with the will of God and Jesus the Christ. I know Christ lives within me. I am secure in God's eternal love.

MAY 3

I am secure in Christ:

I accept the Holy Spirit's presence in this world and hear his voice. I accept the love of God for myself and everyone. The Holy Spirit is my guide and teacher. I am led by the Holy Spirit and know the peace of God. My end is sure and guaranteed by God. What God wills will be done. I am secure in the promises of God.

MAY 4

Peace surrounds me:

I feed good emotions in myself and others, and I starve negative ones. I give thanks in all things and see all challenges of life through the eyes of God and his perfection. I focus on what I want to experience, and I want the peace of God. I never try and conquer others through anger. I am a wise person and respond to all situations with the wisdom of God that lives within me. I do not poison my peace with anger. I concentrate on the qualities I desire. I am loving, kind, and peaceful. There is no fear in me. I live in complete faith in a heavenly Father that never fails. I am at peace.

MAY 5

I am a child of God:

The kingdom of my thoughts is ruled by the king of peace. I am a positive person. I am God's child and heir to his kingdom. My mind is directed by God, and my Father and I are one. I claim my inheritance as his child. I am not possessed by my possessions; my security does not lie in the things of this world. My mind is clear, and I am able to discern God's voice and leading. I am led to make good decisions and have peace with the present moment. I surround each moment with the peace of God.

MAY 6

Today I grow in wisdom:

I am wise and know who I am in Christ. The Holy Spirit is my teacher, and I am constantly learning. I am an honest person and can be trusted. I see every trial as a resurrection opportunity. New life and meaning is given every trial, and God's will is done. I am not attached to the physical things of this world, and I am free of the earth's hold.

MAY 7

God lives within me:

I experience the truths of scripture and increase in inner wisdom daily. I have a partnership with God in everything I do. I am a fit temple for God, and he dwells within me. I recognize and accept my true identity as God's child. I seek wisdom and find it. I apply spiritual truths to my everyday life and experience God's presence in everything that happens. My faith is personal and direct; it is reflected in the way I live. I only follow teachers who manifest truth. I experience God's love in my life.

MAY 8

I see God's light beyond the darkness:

I invoke God's presence and blessing on my life. Light and joy fill my day, and I am one with Christ. I recognize my eternal nature. I crave God in all areas of my life. I am able to see God's presence in all life. I reflect God's love and bring light into darkness. I love those who do not love me, feel for those who do not feel for me, and am generous to those who are only generous to themselves. I express my love through action.

MAY 9

I am host to God:

I keep good company and have good habits. I allow God's light to flow through me, and I am filled with health and life energy. My will is one with God. I am not a slave to things or possessions. My happiness does not depend on stuff. I live plain but think high. I am rich in Spirit. God is absolutely necessary in every area of my life, and I experience his presence. My body is a fit temple for God.

MAY 10

I surround myself with the good in this world:

I cultivate good habits and am filled with good health, success, and wisdom. I have, and seek out good people as friends My friends reflect the good habits I value. My good habits yield good fruit. I hear the inner wisdom within me and cultivate the habit of being good and happy. I know my true worth and attract spiritual results in my life. I cultivate good habits in my life and weed out all the bad. I surround myself with surroundings and circumstances that encourage and build up good habits.

MAY 11

God never leaves me:

I remember God and his image within me. I experience God's perfect presence within me. I am aware of his constant presence in my life. I am able to sense his presence everywhere and never limit his presence or his presents. I am part of the unlimited nature of God and am able to see beyond my earthy body home. I hear God's voice in silence and peace. God's temple is within me. I am able to maintain my inner peace regardless of my circumstances.

MAY 12

I protect the paradise within me and know that:

Nothing of real value will ever perish. My heart has been washed with tears and filled with God's love. My identity rests on God within me. I choose my thoughts carefully and am aware of the power of the mind. I think clearly and calmly, and the Holy Spirit directs my thoughts. God's power within me gives me wisdom, peace, and contentment. I carry my own portable paradise everywhere.

MAY 13

I claim Christ's perfection:

I am filled with enthusiasm, inspiration, and wisdom. I share what I have with others. There is no anger and fear in me. I am healthy and whole. I am filled with thoughts of love and goodwill. I have a secret chamber of silence within me where no inharmony can enter. I meet God in perfection and am happy regardless of my circumstances. I am not a gossip and speak of others to build them up. I offer loving and encouraging words and reflect joy and light into all hearts. My memory of God has been restored, and I am able to see God's presence everywhere.

MAY 14

The seed of God is within me:

I am complete in God. I am part of Christ and the ocean of peace. I seek God first, last, and all the time. I receive all God has given me. My mind is still, and I see God everywhere. I remember my spirit, and it rules my body. I know what is good. I think what is good, and God's goodness is constantly in my thinking. I remember my true nature and am at peace. I am from a seed brought forth from God. I meditate upon the infinite and have an unlimited perspective. My thinking has been transformed and renewed from the physical to the spiritual—the finite to the infinite. I am not limited to the physical body and know myself as Spirit created in God's image. I am God's child and receive him fully as my loving Father. I receive the inheritance he desires me to have.

MAY 15

I can overcome all trials:

I meet every situation from the calm center that is within me. My eternal consciousness brings me joy. I know God is the source of true joy. My soul and mind are cleansed by the tears of Jesus. I am an expression of God's Spirit; my mind is anchored in God. My mind has been resurrected from worldly thinking. Every day I uplift those who are physically, mentally, or spiritually sick. I appreciate God even greater in times of trial. I have the power within me to overcome all trials. I am God's child.

MAY 16

I make good choices today:

I am attached to the spiritual and not the physical. I cultivate good habits. I am God's child and represent him on earth. My body and mind have been healed, and I am part of Christ's wholeness. I live a healthy life and am rewarded by good health. I ask for wisdom and am wise. I ask for prosperity and am spared from poverty. My Spirit is rich in the eternal. Evil tendencies have been burned up within me, and I am God's fit temple. I plant good and loving thoughts and am rewarded. I am surrounded by God's blessings.

MAY 17

I speak health and wholeness over my body:

I have control of my mind and thoughts. I engage in healthy thoughts, activities, and situations. I know the true value of everyone lies in the spiritual. I am able to paint a smile over a gloomy countenance. I choose to be in the company of good people and am constantly improving myself. I am not possessed by my possessions. I remember my true identity as God created me, and I was made in his image. I take pleasure in pleasing God in my daily activities. My mind and body are free of all disease. God is the perfect healer in my life. I accept health and wholeness.

MAY 18

Today I remember:

I am one with the Father, and he knows me as his child. I focus on God's love in my life. I am blessed and am a blessing to others. There is a constant smile within me. I accept God's power within me and radiate wholeness. I keep God's perfect image within me. I help others with my good health, with calmness, courage, good attitude, tolerance, patience, and peace. I focus on God's unchangeable nature and feel peace.

MAY 19

The power of Christ is within me:

My joyful Spirit gives me energy. I do all with deep attention and am in the moment. The joy and cheer in me brings vitality. I am peaceful under all circumstances. God's energy surrounds my body. I give out smiles freely. I am God's employee in everything I do. I am a valuable person and always strive for the best. My most important appointment each day is with God. I choose consciously to do the right thing.

MAY 20
I am a disciple of Christ:

I cultivate good habits. I have inner peace and self-control. I choose to be in the company of good people. I counter all thoughts of darkness with light and life. I model self-control, right living, and proper habits to those around me. I am not a victim of others' anger. I freely forgive and have accepted God's complete forgiveness.

MAY 21
My actions reflect good choices:

I do not gossip about the moral weaknesses of others. I surround myself in a good and healthy environment. The power within me generates self-control, calmness, love, forgiveness, and harmony. Material pleasures have no hold on me. I do not criticize and have banished unkind words from my life. I speak sincere, kind words and am courteous to my family. I am unselfish, wise, calm, meditative, fearless, sweet, sincere, courteous, methodical, true to my word and unafraid to be true, and just.

MAY 22
I make good choices:

I am the person I want others to be. Every moment I practice being secretly happy regardless of my circumstances. I am a magnet attracting spiritual wisdom. I simplify the material realm in my life and broaden the spiritual. I know the spiritual never perishes. I do not waste my time on the perishable. I seek God first. My body is strong and sure, I stand and sit straight. I eat healthy and radiate health. I am a fit temple for God's presence.

MAY 23
I live within a resurrected body:

I am sincere and am able to focus on what I am doing. My mind is clear and clean of toxins. I am a good listener. I always wear the armor of self-control and set a good example. I conquer the ugly and bad with the positive and good. I am able to control my speech and reflect a calm Spirit. I am sweet of speech and thoughtful of others. I never behave unkindly. I reflect the harmony of God within me. I choose carefully my friends. I am influenced by the good people around me. I speak the truth in love. God has healed all my painful memories, and I am set free from the pain of the past. I am resurrected with Christ. All things have been made new.

MAY 24
I am able to lighten my material load as:

My memory is filled with rich treasures. I recall only goodness. My attention is sharp and focused, and I remember God's goodness. I pulverize all negative thoughts from my memory. I know I am God's child, and the power within me is greater than any tests that may come my way. I can and do overcome all tests in life through Christ who lives in me. I focus on the spiritual (eternal) and not the material world. I am less and less attached to the material. I do not grieve for stuff that is taken. My happiness and security is not based on the material world.

MAY 25

Because the power of God is within me:

I have mental freedom regardless of my circumstances. My thoughts are positive. My will and God's will are the same. I am free of bad habits. I possess the power of God within me, and I am filled with his divine current. I reflect God's presence within me. I am always able to control my speech and manner. I react to all ill treatment with forgiveness, especially criticism. I forgive others quickly and completely.

MAY 26

I choose to remember:

I am never alone and comfortless. God lives within me. I am attracted to the goodness of God and am drawn closer to him. My most important appointment is with God. My relationship with God allows me to see the dramas of life through His eyes. My troubles and difficulties help me change for good. I reclaim the forgotten image of God within me and remember my true identity. I am as God created me. I recall my true nature. I love God more than his creations.

MAY 27

My body is free of toxins as:

I meditate on the infinite and know my unity with God. I am able to hear God's voice. My mind is open to truth, and I grow in wisdom. God's song of calmness surrounds me. I do not allow fear to poison my body. I claim God's love for me every time I am tempted to worry. I concentrate on right actions and leave the results to God. I cultivate good habits, and they generate good actions. I claim God's healing power and am whole physically, mentally, and spiritually.

MAY 28

I am part of God's perfect plan:

I constantly develop high moral standards. My close associates reflect those same standards. My soul is united with God. I know God is the power behind everything real, all else is illusion. I recognize God's power and rest in his perfect plan. I am his immortal child. I always wear my best behavior of kindness and a proper attitude. I remain calm and courteous even when disagreeing. No matter what, I behave myself. I don't use harsh words to counter harsh words. I am kind in thought, word, and deed.

MAY 29

I choose to think pure thoughts of others:

My soul is wrapped in peace. I do not blame others. I only give constructive criticism to those who ask for it. I guard myself against mental criticism of myself and others. My mind is cleansed of disturbing thoughts of others. I am a forgiven person, and I forgive others. I don't pity myself when criticized. My family members are all a part of God's divine plan. I am a visible representative of God to my family.

MAY 30

I am able to overcome:

I am not a slave to things or bad habits. I am not a selfish person. I am a member of the human family, of God's children. I see everyone as a brother or sister. I have self-control over my emotions and actions. Christ's power is within me. I am able to control myself in any situation through the power that lives within me.

MAY 31

I am blessed to be a blessing:

The life energy within me is strong and vibrant. The life force from God within me is greater than any physical manifestation. My will wills with God's will. God wills holiness and wholeness. I align my thinking with God. My mind is focused on health and happiness. I think, read, and reflect on God's truth. It is positive, and I am positive. I make those around me happy.

JUNE

JUNE 1

I notice what I am thinking and eating:

I eat right and take proper care of my body. I do not abuse my body in any way. It is a fit temple for God. My body enables me to learn the lessons I need to learn. My mind rejects all toxic thoughts and my cells are healthy and whole. There is no dis-ease in me. My enthusiasm supplies me with fresh energy. I desire wisdom and bliss, harmony and health, and happiness and success for everyone. I keep my mind on the perfect thoughts of God. Peace follows me everywhere.

JUNE 2

I affirm I am created in the image of God:

I reflect God's calmness and peace. My thoughts are filled with love and goodwill. There is no anger in me. I have forgiven all. I don't allow others to upset me. I am peace. I have removed all anger from my heart. God's light reflects throughout my body. I accept his healing perfecting presence. I am well, for perfection lives within me.

JUNE 3

Peace surround me:

I empty my mind of all restless thoughts. God's power flows through me, and I am filled with the healing power of God. My thoughts are good and nourish my body. I surround myself with peaceful thoughts and peaceful friends. Peace penetrates all problems. I have self-control over my eating and relationships. My behavior is honest and economical and brings me peace. My peace is God's altar. I am above all dis-ease—physical, mental, and spiritual. I am God's child and live in his power. I receive God's blessings in my life.

JUNE 4

I focus on health and healing:

Healing power flows within me. God dwells in his perfect sanctuary that is within me. My will is united with God. I am open to the healing rays of God and am healthy and well. I always make good eating choices and live a healthy lifestyle. I willingly give up everything that comes between me and God. I give up material desires for the will of God. I strive for the imperishable.

JUNE 5

The power of God works through me:

I expel all toxic thoughts. I ask for and receive wisdom. My habits and thoughts are based on wise choices. I am led by the Holy Spirit. My Spirit is unchanged. It is as God created it. I remember who I am in Spirit, and I claim my inheritance. God is everywhere, and I experience his presence. My life is sealed in God's will. My spark of Spirit grows brighter and more complete each day. I become more Christlike daily and experience God more fully. I manifest calmness at all times and focus on God's goodness. I accept God's love, wisdom, happiness, health, and prosperity. I accept his care for me.

JUNE 6

God's love and light surround me and bring sunshine into my life:

I am nourished by God's good and perfect gifts. I have good and noble thoughts. I uplift those around me. I am able to see the spiritual beyond the physical and am centered on my Spirit within that never changes. My life has been sealed in God's love. I have self-control in all areas of my life. I do everything as God's representative. I commit my future to God. I rest in his plan and purpose. In stillness, I experience Spirit and know the truth. I remember my thoughts are like words. I choose them carefully and think only those things I am willing to say out loud.

JUNE 7

The Holy Spirit leads me:

I am calm and self-possessed. I accept responsibility for my decisions and don't blame others. I sleep soundly and peacefully. Sleep restores me, and I am energized by life energy. Truth is restored to me, and I know God. I have awakened to the infinite and know that only God is real. I attract good people and good situations into my life. I think and act correctly. I am led by the Holy Spirit and hear his voice. I have a calm mind, and intuition flows through me. I concentrate on Christ within, and answers are given to me. I know the voice of God and receive his guidance. My mind is clear and an open vessel for God's use. Peace is mine.

JUNE 8

My words and thoughts reflect God's love:

My heart is filled with love for God, and I am filled with inner peace. I remember my divine identity. I constantly affirm my love for God and know I am his child. I know God, and he is my loving Father. My nature has been purified, and I am in control of my moods. I do not criticize others and have removed criticizing thoughts from my mind. I speak kind words only. God is working through me. I am powered by God's life force. I keep it pure and use it for his purposes. I am filled with the wisdom of God and hear his voice. My mind and body are strong.

JUNE 9
I affirm my real identity:

I affirm the truth because I know who I am in Christ. I know my true nature as God's child. God's kingdom of silence is within me. I am powered by his presence. I use healing words and words of peace. I am part of the infinite Spirit of God. My will is guided by God's will, and there is no doubt and fear in me. I am free of pain, and all dis-ease has been uprooted in my life. I accept the perfect peace of God. My mind is ever awake in God. My soul is enclosed in Spirit; it is not limited to the physical ego. My true identity is Spirit and not body.

JUNE 10
Peace surrounds me:

I sleep soundly and peacefully. I use my will to do God's will. I am guided by God's wisdom. I focus on the positive and see God's guiding hand in the everyday events. I give my will to divine will. I speak and think positive thoughts. I remain inwardly calm under all circumstances. I know God is with me. I am never alone.

JUNE 11
I remember:

I am a blessed child of God. I am his representative in this world. God's light shines on everyone and everything. I reflect God's light to the world. I am awake to truth, and wisdom flows through me. I eat good healthy food and radiate health. I set a good example for those around me. God's consciousness flows through me. I see God's image within me and know perfection. I am peace, satisfaction, safety, conscious knowledge, and immortality. I see God's perfect image being manifested in human life. I am a part of the great ocean of life. I am not an isolated wave. All others and I are God's children. We are part of God and his eternal plan.

JUNE 12

I grow daily in wisdom:

I am free of all physical entanglements. My focus is on God who lives within me and gives me life. God's love and light are reflected through me. I am calm and concentrate with full attention. I think and act with a clear mind. My thoughts are filled with wisdom, and wisdom controls my actions. I sow good seeds into the soil of my life. I do not misuse the free will given to me by God. My choices conform to God's will. I perform the most important, useful, and necessary duties of life first and concentrate until they are done. God's wisdom manifests itself in my life. I accept my birthright as a child of God.

JUNE 13

I am resurrected with Christ:

All limitations of the soul have been freed in my Spirit awareness. My mind is open to truth, and I willingly live the truth. Jesus lives through me. I am able to face any tests of life. I am strong in Christ. My mind is focused on God's power and wholeness within me. God is greater than any tests this life can hand me. I see beyond my soul-body and accept and live in my Spirit freedom. I am as God created me. I am released from all false illusions and am rooted in God's truth. All fear is dispelled by faith.

JUNE 14

God's presence gives me peace:

I am awakened to his presence within me. I am not imprisoned in the physical world. My consciousness and energy flows down from God. I remember my true identity and immortality and know the truth about myself. I am God's beloved child, completely accepted by him. I see myself as God sees me—loved and loveable. My love and God's love are not limited. I am able to see the light of God within me. I rest in my eternal home. My mind is a compass always facing God. I am not attached to matter but the eternal. I am victorious on the physical battlefields of good and evil. I focus on the unchangeable and eternal. I see beyond the delusion of the temporal.

JUNE 15

I am blessed:

I remember that God is always patient with me. God is always kind to me. God does not envy. He does not boast. He is not proud. God is not rude to me. He is not self-seeking. God keeps no records of my wrongs and rejoices with the truth. He always protects me and always perseveres with me. God's love for me will never fail. My suffering from evil has awakened me to wisdom. Love destroys evil; it is always stronger than evil. The wisdom within me is stronger than the temptations of this world. My present actions are based on bringing future blessings. My actions today are based on the Holy Spirit's leading. I reject all evil and bad habits and embrace good thoughts and healthy life choices. I ask for God's help, and he hears my needs. I am secure in his love for me.

JUNE 16

Peace surrounds me:

There is no anger and jealousy in me. I forgive as God forgave me. I am not attached to the material of this world but focus on the eternal. God is my provider, and I depend on him. God's immortal arms surround me with love. The riches of God are immortal and imperishable. I choose today good actions in everything I do. God shows me the way out of all difficulties. I am not selfish but generous with what God has given me. I purge myself of material luxury and am decorated with the knowledge, wisdom, and love of God. I live simply and do not concentrate on unnecessary things. I am in the world but not of the world. My mind is stayed on God.

JUNE 17

I am a magnet for good in this world:

I draw good people toward me. My body is free of poisons and toxins, and God's energy flows though me freely. My mind is clear and thinks health. God's power flows through me. I reflect God's power within me to the world. I surround myself with good company and good environments that build up my inner environment. My body is a fit temple for God's presence. I learn from the trials of life and become wiser. I improve myself daily and do not allow the actions of others to dictate my happiness. My peace of mind is based on God's love for me and not my circumstances.

JUNE 18

I freely accept God's blessings and know:

I am part of the consciousness of God. I see beyond the body and know I am Spirit. I remember my eternal nature and am sustained by God. God's mercy and love is poured out daily into my life. I see his love and protection in my life. In silence, I hear God and am calm. God reveals truth to me. I ask for wisdom, and it is given to me. God's timeless wisdom is restored to me. I know and experience God's love for me. All my actions are dedicated to God. His arms of tranquility are locked around me, and I rest in his care.

JUNE 19

I put my trust in God:

I am free of fear. I include God in all my actions. I release my will to the will of God and am part of his divine plan. My right thinking brings right action. My good thoughts nourish my mind. I focus on good thoughts and am at peace. God's image is within me and draws me back to my eternal home. I love God above all else. I sow good seeds into my life, and God produces good results. My life is part of God's divine plan and has purpose.

JUNE 20
I acknowledge the Christ within me:

The veil of ignorance has been torn, and I know I have been resurrected in Christ. My mind is stayed on God, and his healing power flows through me. The mighty power of God draws me back to him. The love and light of God fills my life. The wisdom within me keeps me from evil, and I am part of God's divine will. The life force within me is strong and healthy. I make choices that keep me from suffering. My protection comes from God. I am master over my emotions and choose to make wise decisions. I am not tempted by material and temporal pleasures. My security and strength rests in God's love for me.

JUNE 21
I see the good in this world:

I am not a critical person. I see the good in others. Christ consciousness lets me see through the eyes of Jesus. My true prosperity lies in the divine will within me. God is the provider of all I need. My security rests in the arms of God. I live simply and am calm. I am able to hear God's voice. My mind and body are healthy and whole. They are fit temples for God's presence. I surround myself with a good and healthy environment that encourages good habits.

JUNE 22

I am worthy and accepted completely:

My center rests in God's causeless Spirit. I am not controlled by negative habits. The spiritual force within me is stronger than any physical force around me. God reveals the truth of Scripture to me. I realize truth, not just know about truth. Christ lives in me. I am resurrected with Jesus; I am a new creation in Christ. I accept what was done for me and live wholly acceptable to God.

JUNE 23

My security comes from God:

I am secure in the shelter of God. I am safe forever. I experience God's love and provision every day. My consciousness has been dissolved into Christ consciousness. I see as God sees. My Father and I are one. I am not attached to the matter of this world. I choose spiritual sight over physical sight. I choose the eternal over the physical and material. I am filled with God's healing power. My mind, body, and spirit are filled with the flaming energy of God. All negative thoughts have been burned in the fire of fear. My mind is filled with faith and freedom.

JUNE 24

I am a healed person:

Peace and harmony surround me, and I know my true nature as a child of God. I am unconditionally loved and accepted by God. I am God's divine child. My will and energy flow through Christ within me. My thoughts are impregnated with the will of God. My healthy will overcomes the negative things of this world. My soul of ignorance has been healed, and I accept my identity with Christ. My soul knows its divine nature, and I am filled with divine energy. My will is guided by wisdom and God's will.

JUNE 25

I acknowledge the divine within me:

God's healing energy is running through my body. Divine gravitation is constantly pulling me back to God. My mind is brightened by God's presence. His infinite nature is revealed to me, and I know the infinite nature of my soul. I am one with the eternal. I am not bound by the material. I hold all my possessions with open hands. My possessions do not possess me. I destroy mortal thoughts by immortal thoughts. I am part of the vast ocean of life. My entire body is impregnated with the thoughts of God. I am part of God's eternal nature and his perfect plan. I live in peace. I am his beloved child.

JUNE 26

Daily I become more aware of God's presence within me:

The seed of God is everywhere waiting to grow. I am quiet and know his presence. I meditate on his presence within me and remember our oneness. I am part of the ocean of all life that never dies. My only ambition is to know God. I see God in everyone and in all creation. God allows me to see as he sees. Every night, I surrender myself completely to God. God is the only reality. I place my thoughts under God's control. God's presence fills all my thoughts, and I am strong in character. The kingdom of heaven is within me.

JUNE 27

The power of God within me empowers me:

I kill all fear by knowing I am part of God's eternal plan. I am protected by his love and know his peace. God is a part of everything I do. I use my time and income wisely. I do not overcommit or overspend. I am able to counter the wrong feelings of others with kind feelings in my heart. Love is able to vibrate through me. I am always conscious of being with God. His peace and presence guides me and fills me with hope.

JUNE 28

I live forever in Christ:

I pass the mortal tests of time. I overcome in Christ and am drawn back to the Father. I exchange my free will for his goodwill. I am part of God's cosmic pull drawing me home. I have been raised with Christ and accept my rightful place as his child. My body, mind, and soul are filled with the consciousness of Christ. All ignorance in me has been crucified, and I am resurrected to truth. I love all as God loves. Christ's consciousness shines through me.

JUNE 29
I nurture the timeless within me:

I live wisely and do not judge others. I do not expose others faults in public. I do not criticize or advise others unless asked. I love those who love and also hate me. My inner being is a place of beauty. My smiles come from deep within. My center is calm. I live with hope and, as God's child, know nothing is too good for me. God's image within me has been restored to my consciousness. God within brings faith without. I share God's reality with those around me. I am sealed in an unchangeable truth.

JUNE 30
God's grace surrounds me:

I cultivate wisdom and make good choices. I am Spirit-led and hear the voice of the Holy Spirit. I see others in a positive and loving way. My strong will and self-discipline allows me to change any bad habit, personality flaws, or deep-rooted errors. God's seed is within me. I cultivate my relationship with God and know his presence in my life. I am an overcomer. I always choose God's way over the world's way. I live in the wholeness and health of God. There is no dis-ease in me. My identity rests in God's will, and I am secure.

JULY

JULY 1

I focus on the presence of God:

I live in the *now*. I see God's presence everywhere but value the unseen above the seen. The vibration of God's will is present in all matter. I unite my consciousness with God and know the real from the dream of delusion. I reclaim my birthright and see everything as one consciousness of God. I am a perpetual inhabitant of eternity. My security rests on a solid plan of God. I practice the presence of God daily and choose to be happy.

JULY 2

I remember truth:

God is constantly on my mind. I am free from bad moods and bad habits. The power of Christ lives within me, and I am free. My mind is awake to truth. I see though the eyes of Christ, and true sight is restored. I am able to see through my spiritual eye and remember truth. My consciousness is restored, and I know I am God's child held in his immortal arms. My future is secure, and I can never be lost.

JULY 3

I am free in Christ:

I am not attached to the things of this earth. My mind is open to the eternal, and God consciousness pervades all my actions and moods. I claim a resurrected consciousness and my relationship with the infinite. I am restored in my mind and know I am the pure reflected image of Spirit. I have been purified with Christ. I reestablish my identity with Spirit. I am awake to my eternal nature and live my life above the physical plane. I am spiritually strong. I am free of wrong thinking and wrong actions. I am resurrected from the ungodly. God's power within prepares me for any kind of trial or test. God's peace and love covers every situation.

JULY 4

Today is a new beginning:

I am free from my past and today live free in my resurrected body. I am resurrected with Christ and am not bond to my body. My life is lived through Christ. My thoughts are pure and worthy of the eternal. I hear God's voice and know I am loved and accepted. I am one with the infinite flame of life *now*. God reveals himself to me. God within allows me to see God everywhere. My life is upheld by the ocean of all life. Peace and rest are mine.

JULY 5

I choose to make good choices:

I eat healthy and live in a harmonious environment. I surround myself with good books, good company, and good thoughts. I meditate on who I am in Christ. My body, mind, and spirit are whole, healthy, and holy as God created me. My soul is healed of delusion, and God's truth lives through me. I focus on the inner me that never changes and is timeless. I live less on food and more on God's energy within. God's love draws everything back to him. There is no fear in me. God is in control. All fear has been uprooted in me, and I am protected by the battlements of God's eternal safety. Nothing that happens can harm my eternal self.

JULY 6

The Light of God surrounds me:

I eliminate all hindrances to divine harmony in me. All darkness is replaced by God's healing light. God's power freely flows through me. Each day is a new birth in which I choose to resurrect the body, mind, and soul. My daily duties are done with the consciousness of God. I have overcome the world and am a pillar in God's presence. My soul is fixed on God.

JULY 7
I accept my true identity:

My decisions today prepare me for a great future. I accept Jesus's perfect soul. I replace my ego with identity with Christ. Earthly desires have been eliminated and replaced with spiritual wisdom. My soul's desire is to inherit the eternal kingdom. I am in the world but not of the world. My identity is eternal. I possess self-control, detachment from the material, morality, calmness, and spirituality that endures. I am no longer tied to earthly desires.

JULY 8
God is my guide:

My love for God is greater than all else. I grow in divine love that is unselfish and unconditional. I perform all actions with the consciousness of God. God's throne of calmness reigns within me. I am God's willing instrument, and he works through me. I am guided by God who never fails. I smile through any storms of suffering. Wisdom brings me through the sea of trials, and my mental ship is aimed at God.

JULY 9
God embraces me with his love:

Christ's compassion cures cause and effect. I am set free from the past, and I accept my true identity. I am God's child—loved, loveable, and accepted. I plant good seeds (actions) and produce good fruit (results). The parasite of sin has been removed from my soul. Evil tendencies in me have been destroyed, and the past no longer controls me. My soul has been liberated, and I accept my freedom in Christ. I am enveloped in God's all-protecting omnipresence in birth, in sorrow, in joy, in death. Nothing can separate me from the love of God.

JULY 10
I can depend on the promises of God:

I focus on God's changelessness. I feel God's power flowing into my body and live by his grace. My mind controls my body and not the body the mind. My mind is stayed on God and eternal truths. I serve myself good psychological menus, and my mind is filled with healthy thoughts. Every day, I become stronger in body, mind, and soul. I surround myself with good company, sound reasoning, and mental discipline. Wisdom flows through me and brings me peace. I concentrate on those things that are absolutely necessary. I know the difference between needs and wants. I am filled with real prosperity that only comes from God. I practice the presence of peace, and God's power flows though me. My mind is a diamond that God's light shines through. I seek God first in all things. I choose spiritual abundance and experience God's blessings in my life.

JULY 11
I am part of God's eternal plan:

I follow God's laws of physical, mental, and spiritual harmony. I do not pass judgment on others. I watch my thoughts carefully and am free of bad habits. I choose my friends carefully and listen to God's whisper in my consciousness. God uses my voice to speak his words. I learn valuable lessons from my experiences. I do not repeat wrong actions. I learn from my errors. When lessons are learned, I scatter the memories in the wind. I remember the good, the loving, and the kind. I remember all are children of God. I am part of God's eternal plan and know I am safe and secure in Spirit. I am able to see God in everyone and everything.

JULY 12

I am becoming more aware of God's presence within me:

God is waking my sleeping soul and wisdom in being poured into my mind. I remember Spirit, and I remember my birthright. Divine consciousness is restored. I recognize God within me. God is the architect of my life. I surrender my will to his will. I act on and live God's truths. My first priority is to know God. I see beyond the temporal matter to eternal Spirit. As ripe fruit falls from a tree, so will I pass on when I am complete.

JULY 13

I give up material desires for the eternal:

I sleep in the cradle of God's eternal calm. I awaken to immortal wakefulness in God. The secreted temple of heaven is revealed to me. I remember God and am free of material desires. God's presence is my one desire, and I know myself perfectly as a reflection of God. In stillness,

I know the truth. I am reborn from "I" to omnipresent—I am made in God's image.

JULY 14

God's pure energy flows through me:

Health and wholeness fills my body. My soul is encased in God's eternal energy. I am filled with goodness, self-control, a calm spirit, love, good habits, and forgiveness. Christ has been reborn into my consciousness. I do my best and leave the rest to God. I direct my will in accordance with God's will. I live in the present and am not burdened by the past or the future. The altar of my heart has been washed by the tears of repentance. The resurrected Christ lives through me, filling me with health, self-control, happiness, and peace.

JULY 15

I am not separated from the Spirit:

God's Spirit is within me, and I am led by the Spirit. I hear the voice of the Holy Spirit and am drawn to the finite. I associate with desirable people and absorb their good qualities. I mediate and visualize on the spiritual within and without. I see God's expression everywhere and am God's divine magnet. My peace and happiness is secure, and I allow no one to take it away. I am calm and open the door to God's presence. Divine love surrounds me and is the magnet that draws God's goodness to me.

JULY 16

Each day determines each tomorrow:

I love *now* the best I can. I soak in the inner peace of God's presence. My body is not enslaved to the environment. I am first and foremost Spirit. I choose carefully whom I associate with. I have a good effect on others, and others do not infect me. My peace and happiness are held in God's hand—my mind is stayed on God.

JULY 17

My quiet and calm nature allows me to experience God within:

Divine love draws all good to me. I am lifted above the physical and know I am Spirit. My body is not enslaved to my environment. I am Spirit and a part of God's unity. My soul is made in the image of God. I am in control of my ego and feelings through the power of Christ that lives within me. I monitor my thoughts carefully and focus on the results I desire. I reject the inharmonious ideas of others and focus on God's omnipresence. Pain is my friend that warns me when I have gone astray. I have replaced all physical desires for spiritual desires.

JULY 18

The vibration of my words is sweet and worthy:

I send out only what I want returned. I direct my energy toward health and wholeness. Nothing rules me unless I let it. I do not judge others. The power within me is greater than my problems. I choose carefully the choices I make and keep good company. I am surrounded by a hedge of good habits. I allow God to express himself through me. I pray the Father's will be done in my life.

JULY 19

My mind is open to the sacred:

My ignorance was crucified with Christ and truth was resurrected in me. God is drawing all creation back to him through love and free will. My mind is my servant and not my master. I possess all that I need—the sacred lives within me. My true nature is being revealed to me in silence. I am able to recognize the true from the false. I see the seed of God in everyone. I am able to hear the voice of the Holy Spirit within me and remember truth. I do not limit or try and contain God. I am enlightened to the degree I desire it. In peace and quiet, I know God and seek first the kingdom of God. Direct experience of the divine is librating. I am led by Spirit and am liberated.

JULY 20

I focus on healthy emotions:

I use my mind; it does not use me. I am able to discern false thoughts from truth. I put away all false thoughts and live in God's truth. I have given Spirit control of my mind and am filled with God's positive energy. Each second, I am born again. I live in the present and am reconnected to the Spirit within me. My emotions are under the control of Spirit and are healthy. My body reflects the healthy emotions inside me. I have released and forgiven the past and trust God with the future. I can feel my emotions without being controlled by them. I am the interested observer of my emotions and not a slave to them.

JULY 21

The light of God is my guide:

I experience God's love, joy, and peace beyond my circumstances. I accept what is *now* and make the most of the present moment. I work with the present as if I had chosen it. I am full of positive energy, and all pain has been removed. All past pain has been brought to the light and no longer has a hold on me. I only feel good emotions. I choose to starve negative emotions and pain, and they die. God's love and light has removed all darkness from my life. I identify and give strength to the eternal. My inner space is sanctified by God's presence.

JULY 22

I eliminate anger by releasing the pain beneath it:

I accept God's image of me, and my words reflect that identity. I crucify my ego daily and live through the Spirit within me. God's internal presence rules my life. I am not a slave to the external. I am a child of God and trust God for the present moments in my life. I learn from my mistakes, then move on. I accept God's forgiveness and am released from the past. I accept the present moment without regret.

JULY 23

I live in the present as a present from God:

I accept salvation from the past and assurance for the future *now*. I accept what *is* in the spiritual and make good choices in all the *now* moments of my life. I am able to overcome or accept all the situations and challenges in my life. I do the right thing and leave the results to God. I accept myself just as I am right now—whole and complete in Christ. I am not my ego and know that nothing real can be threatened. God's truth about me is real. I am able to discern thoughts of the ego from thoughts of the Spirit. I am Spirit-led. I do not allow difficult people and situations to derail me from living in Spirit. I practice the presence of peace and am strong enough to weather the storms of life. God's light always eliminates the darkness.

JULY 24

I set my mind—my mind does not set me:

I produce the emotions I desire, and they reflect my inner peace. I am constantly cleaning my inner being of all toxic thoughts. I do not contaminate my body with negative thoughts, actions, and words. I am one of the branches in God's tree of life. I bring fresh air to the spaces I inhabit and leave a pleasant scent. I am doing my part to clean up this world, and it begins with my inner world.

JULY 25

I keep only the worthy in my life:

I release myself of all useless baggage. Behind everything—God is. I willingly give up all actions, food, or emotions that make me sick. I am not a victim and do not complain. I willingly change my attitude to maintain peace within. I surrender to God what I can't change. I live in the present and have died to the past. I do not allow the future to rob me of the present and hear God's answers in the *now*. My good choices now produce good *now* moments in the future.

JULY 26

I focus on truth—I am created in the image of God:

I see beyond my physical errors and accept my inheritance. God has given me all I will ever need. I give up all the idols of this world for truth. I am powered by Spirit and not mind. Life allows me to know and experience truth. I listen to the stillness within me, and Christ is revealed. The truth sets me free to experience the dimensions of eternity on earth. Christ lives through me.

JULY 27

I give up all labels and disguises I have assumed:

I claim my spiritual birthright and know I am God's child. My body and mind are controlled by Spirit and are healthy and whole. The sanctuary of my mind is a place of peace. I guard my mind from the free will of error. I focus on the eternal and not the temporal. My inner strength is the bridge that takes care of the every day. Nothing is outside of God's plan. I am firmly rooted in the eternal that lives within me. I reveal all negative emotions to the light and their darkness disappears. I am quick to forgive and am not burdened by an unforgiving Spirit. My immune system is strong and free of unwanted guests. I flood my body with Christ consciousness. My life energy comes from God, and I focus on its perfection.

JULY 28
Stillness and peace lie at my core:

I rest in God's power that lives within me. I am the bridge between God and the world. I focus on my inner spirit that is timeless. I am exactly as God created me. My inner being lacks nothing. I recognize the unmanifested around me, and my faith in God grows stronger. I no longer blame or pass judgment. I lead a quiet and peaceful life and remove all that keeps me from hearing the Holy Spirit. In silence, I know. I notice the "no-thing" that opens the pathway to purity of consciousness. God is in the stillness. The truth of the unmanifested fills me with peace.

JULY 29
Nothing real is ever lost:

I affirm my true self as God created me. I accept all that I am as God created me right now. Everything that ever was is mine in this very moment. I accept every gift and attribute God planned for me and my inheritance as his child. I am rich and wise in the eternal. My completeness comes from who I am in Christ and not my worldly relationships. I am not addicted to anyone or anything of this world. I release all pain that is in me. The pain of the past has been healed by the present. I notice my thoughts and behavior and place them under the control of the Holy Spirit. My false self (ego) has no control over me. I live through the freedom I have in Christ.

JULY 30

We are all one in Christ:

I see beyond the external. The veil of form and separation has been lifted from my eyes. I notice God's holy presence in myself and others. God's love flows through me. I allow God to work and live in my life. My decisions are based on God's will and presence within me. I use unpleasant relationships and situations as spiritual practices. I hold others' bad behavior in God's loving embrace. I accept others as God accepts them. My actions are conscious and not reactions to unconscious behavior. I choose how I respond to every situation. Christ's perfect presence lives within me, and his power allows me to overcome the world. I am one with Christ. I do not judge but am a light in this world. God's light flows through me. I dispel the darkness in others with my light within. I do not blame, accuse, or attack other people. There is no place in my life for a critical spirit— Christ's consciousness lives through me.

JULY 31

The present is more powerful than the past:

I am a bridge between the manifested and unmanifested world—between the physical and the spiritual. Pain, emotional and physical, no longer rules me. The pain of the past has been burned in God's refining fire. I take responsibility for my inner space where God resides. I do not allow the past to be more powerful in my life than the present. I feed my Spirit and not my ego. I am an intricate ripple in the ocean of God. I am part of the whole and not an isolated wave. My completeness comes as being a part of God's wholeness—all that exist. I use unhappiness as an opportunity to awaken. I accept each moment fully. I accept myself fully. I do not confuse my ego with my true self. I see myself and others through the eyes of Christ. My inner peace does not depend on the conditions of my life.

AUGUST

AUGUST 1

I learn from the lessons of life:

Often my most negative experiences are my greatest teachers. I look for the lesson behind all negativity and pain that comes into my life. I am a good student and learn the lessons of life. God works all things together for his perfect plan. I work and walk through the negative and become wiser. I forgive each moment I perceive as negative. There is no accumulation of toxic thoughts in me. All resentment has been released, and I am healthy in body, mind, and spirit. Only goodness lives within me. I am filled with the peace of God. I accept who I am through Christ. God meets all my needs.

AUGUST 2

My life is rooted in hope.

I replace good for harm in all situations. I affirm God's presence in the physical, psychological, and spiritual by my words and actions. There is nothing beyond God's control, and His divine plan is in effect. I reinforce and reaffirm the existence of Spirit in all my thoughts, words, and deeds. I travel through my day with fruitful thoughts, I chose hope over hopelessness, and Spirit grows stronger in me. I purge all thoughts of fear from my thinking and replace them with hope.

AUGUST 3

I do not attract negative drama into my life:

I relinquish all resistance and accept what is and forgive all. My ability to forgive frees me from all suffering in Spirit. All evil in my life has been redeemed through forgiveness. I am born again in every situation and choose again. My past decisions do not have a hold on the present. The ego of yesterday no longer rules me. I interact with the egos around with the Spirit within me. I am free of drama, conflict, power struggles, and emotional and physical violence. I no longer feel sorry for myself, feel guilty, or am anxious. I have given up all drama that creates illness and dis-ease. I am covered by the peace of God.

AUGUST 4

I counter all suffering with acceptance:

I express myself without a negative, reactive force behind my comments. I hold firm to the unchangeable within me—the peace of God that is not dependent on my circumstances. I see the spiritual lesson behind everything the world classifies as bad. I thank God for the failures, loss, and pain that draw me back to God. I hold all things in my life with open hands. I am able to let go of everything that keeps me from God. I willingly surrender the things, people, and circumstances that keep me from wholeness and God's righteousness. I am not my external circumstances. I am a part of the timeless and formless, and my spiritual beauty can never age. My identity rests in the eternal. God is the architect of my life, and his plans are perfect. My security does not lie in the external. I live out of my core of peace. I counter all negativity by nonresistance. I dissolve negative situations by acceptance, forgiveness, and focusing on the positive. Negative thoughts are pollutants and poisons, and I do not allow them to put toxins in my body. I release all toxic thoughts and live in peace.

AUGUST 5

I do not allow the irritations of life to build up and harden on my soul:

I allow all negativity to flow through me. I rise above the circumstances I find myself in and don't allow others to control my inner state. I give out what I want. I choose to react from my inner reality and not the outer. God lives in the quiet, undisturbed within me, and I look beyond the surface situations in my life. I see beyond the parts we play to the true being—as God created us. True vision is restored to me.

AUGUST 6

I expect the best and see the best:

The unconscious behavior of others flows through me. My roots are planted in the spiritual and the freedom I have in Christ. I am free of the fear of loss and securely grounded in Christ. I claim each moment as the peaceful present and teach others through peace. I allow peace to flow into everything I do. I have no enemies. My inner peace is reflected in my physical presence. I bring peace to this world.

AUGUST 7

All my needs are met by God:

My forgiveness to others allows me to accept forgiveness from God. Suffering and pain can be my most convincing teachers. Each moment is another chance to be born again from the past. I combat ego issues with spiritual strength. I do not create my own drama by my thoughts. My self-talk brings peace to me and those around me. I resist all arguments but hold fast to the truth. I make my point without being reactive. I am grounded by the unchangeable within me—the peace of God—and that will never change. My life situation does not identify me. I am not my external conditions, be it financial, physical, or social. I know who I am in eternity. I allow God to flow my life down the river of life, and I accept where it takes me. I live in a state of grace.

AUGUST 8

I am a positive person:

I look for God's guiding hand behind all I see and experience. My positive attitude weakens my ego. I focus on the positive and experience good health. I learn my lessons from life and move forward. I acknowledge any negativity, irritations, and pain, then move on to the present moment that is another chance to begin again. I am able to rise above the circumstances I find myself in and am not a victim to others' behavior. I give out what I wish to receive. I desire peace and surrender all non-peaceful situations in my life.

AUGUST 9

I look for and see the best in my life:

I see through spiritual eyes that look beyond the physical. God leads me in the decisions I make. I ask for God's wisdom in all I do. I enjoy the pleasures of this world with open hands. Fear of loss has no control over me. The physical has no real value, and the spiritual can never be lost or taken. I focus on the unchangeable. I feed my soul daily, and it grows in strength and wisdom. I practice living a peaceful present. I surrender all lies I have believed about myself to God. I am as he created me, and I accept my true identity.

AUGUST 10

I yield to the flow of life and recognize God's presence:

I accept each moment and take action from a positive, mental attitude. I do not judge others, and all tension and rigidity in me have been released. I accept what is happening in my life and then act to achieve change if needed. I align myself with God's plan, then take appropriate action. I focus on the one thing I can do now.

AUGUST 11

I am free of hidden resentments:

My mind has been cleansed of all negativity, and I surrender to God's will for my life. I choose to do things God's way. My thinking comes from the Spirit within me and not my ego. I appreciate each moment, and my spiritual energy is strong. I am aware of God's presence in every situation and don't allow others to use or manipulate me. I am able to say no without attacking the negatives. I choose inner peace in every unpleasant experience. My life is held in God's hands.

AUGUST 12

I accept people the way they are:

I do not use other people. I surrender my egos need to be right in the eyes of others. Being right needs no justification. I defuse the short fuses in other people and bring a calming peace to those around me. My strength comes from surrendering to God's perfect will.

I accept who I am in Christ and live above my outward circumstances. My outward circumstances are aligning with God's perfect will. My faith grows stronger daily and is transforming my mind and circumstances. I put my faith in action, and it grows.

AUGUST 13
I do not label myself or others:

I reject all false identity in myself and others. I live a life of surrendering to truth and not the lies of this world. My identity and life is secure in Christ. All negative situations allow me the opportunity to become present in the moment and move beyond my ego. I have crucified my old life and been reborn into a new life. I am able to see beyond the world's definitions and truth—God's divine plan. I have surrendered my ego for God's way.

AUGUST 14
My days are filled with God's grace:

The fires of life refine me and allow me to be all that God intended. I remove all Band-Aids from my pain and expose it to the healing power of surrender to God. I experience true healing that removes the source. I deal with all pain until I have released it to full acceptance and complete surrender. My inner self is filled with God's healing and loving light. Each breath I take is a new beginning. My past does not define my future as I place the present in God's loving hands. All things are possible through God who loves and cares for me. I choose the peace of God within me in every circumstance.

AUGUST 15

I crucify my ego daily and live through the Spirit of God within me:

I choose God's image of me and not the worlds. The power of God lives through me. I choose God's peace in every situation. God's love for me draws me back to his perfect plan for me. I constantly make a conscious decision to see things God's way. My future and present are secure in God. I surrender my thoughts, actions, and attitudes to the Spirit within me.

AUGUST 16

I accept true forgiveness for myself:

I am free from the past and accept God's total acceptance and love for me now. God restores my memory, and right thinking is restored in my mind. I am free from the egos lies and am healed of all errors. I see God's hand in the people and circumstances around me. I can discern the truth from the false, and I don't take the false seriously. I choose my thoughts carefully based on the results I want. I search for what I want to find. My thinking determines my emotions, and I choose God's way. I know I will become what I think. I always choose Spirit-thinking over ego-thinking. I know that just because I think something and think it to be true, does not necessarily make it true. I have power over my thoughts. My positive thoughts create positive feelings.

AUGUST 17

God's wisdom is within me:

I choose God's view of every situation and remember my spiritual dimension. I have positive thoughts and therefore have positive feelings. I have childlike faith in my heavenly Father. I access my inner wisdom and am filled with compassion, gratitude, and love. I have removed the false filters that distort and cause me to judge. I see myself and others through Christ's eyes. God's design is on my life. I choose to think positively in spite of my circumstances. I am constantly making better choices in my life and planting better memories for the future. I react from God's Spirit within me and not my ego. Thinking with God is filled with compassion, gratitude, humor, understanding, and love. I see through spiritual eyes. I ask for and receive truth from God in every situation and challenge. I remember that within every difficult situation lies opportunity for solutions, growth, and miracles.

AUGUST 18

I replace all judgment with love:

I reject everything that impedes my spiritual progress. I am God's thought and have been made in his image. I have a quiet body and mind and am an open vehicle to accept wisdom and common sense. My mind is a clean space open to show love, understanding, compassion, forgiveness, and gratitude. I counter all low moods with gratitude. I am the master through Christ over my thoughts and not a slave. I have been resurrected with Christ, and his power is within me. I can do all things through the power that lives within me.

AUGUST 19

I learn from my mistakes, then move on:

Learning allows me to move on from painful experiences. I am a good student and learn what I need to know. I apply my learning to my life and share my lessons with others when asked. I am worthy regardless of worldly success or failure; my worth is decided and has been decided by God and will never change. I believe God's truth about me and not the lies of the world. I use my feelings to get back on track. Wrong feelings result from wrong thoughts. I pay attention to what I am thinking. I surrender my thoughts to God.

AUGUST 20

I live with an attitude of gratitude:

I believe in the power of the unseen and am able to look beyond my physical circumstances. The world's ways are not God's way. I believe in God's evaluation of me, and his grace extends over every part of my life. Nothing is outside of his acceptance of me. I quiet my mind, and I know God's truth. Inner wisdom and inspiration flows though me, and I am an open source for God's truths in this world. I focus on God's peace within me.

AUGUST 21

I seek soul knowledge and not head knowledge only:

I use outward information as a source of learning and spiritual growth. I surrender thoughts and attitudes that keep me from God's best for me. I ask for and receive God's insight to see positively. I accept this present moment as God's present to me and thank him for it. I am grateful for this *now* moment in my life. I release all the trash in my mind and life, and I live a life of clarity and simplicity. My mind is a clean screen for God to write on; all trash has been released and removed forever. My mind is a place of peace. God is in control.

AUGUST 22

Common sense, wisdom, and inspiration fill my mind:

My mind is programmed with God. My security and self-worth rests in God's loving hands. My inner wisdom and inspiration allows me to make good choices, and I live a life of God-given principles. My peace of mind is contagious, and I do not allow my circumstances to rob me of my inner peace. I always choose God's peace over the ways of the world. I forgive everyone, and the peace of God fills those voids. I look for and see God's loving hand at work in this world. I rest in the promise of his perfect plan.

AUGUST 23

I am a positive person and keep positive thoughts:

I notice what I am thinking and use my thoughts to keep me on the right track. I take charge of my thoughts, and my thoughts are not allowed to take charge of me. I can do all things through Christ who lives in me. I claim the power within me to overcome. I am true to myself and do not sacrifice myself to the expectations of others. I do not compromise my inner wisdom to please the world. I am open to the inner wisdom of others and grow in Spirit.

AUGUST 24

I am a forgiving person:

I hear the voice of God within me and do not compromise my inner wisdom. I am important because I am a child of God. Achievements and possessions have nothing to do with my worth. I die to my ego daily and live through Spirit-leading. I do not allow the faulty thinking of the ego to lead me astray. Inner wisdom leads me. I forgive others their faulty egos and am released of anger. I do not justify anger but forgive its source. My thinking, talking, and actions reflect forgiveness and not anger. God's peace fills me.

AUGUST 25

I thank God for this moment:

I claim his working in all the circumstances of my life and know he is in control. His perfect plan has overcome the world. I think from Spirit and not the flesh. I choose to look at every situation through the eyes of Christ. I do not support false interpretations in myself or others. I speak the truth in love. My baggage from the past has been burned in God's refining fire. I see the positive in every situation and give thanks. I know that to complain, I remain. I do not complain but move forward in God's plan for my life.

AUGUST 26

I look for the positive, and my emotions respond accordingly:

I allow God's peace to fill my body with health and wholeness. It is not my job to change other people; it is just my job to not hinder God's plan. Unconditional love looks past insecure behavior. God's unconditional love flows through me. I claim the inner peace of God regardless of my physical circumstances. I share my inner peace with those around me and reflect God's love for me.

AUGUST 27

God is in the gap between my expectations and my now *moments:*

In every situation, I replace stress with Spirit-thinking. I do not choose the world's ways but rely on God's truth. I claim his working plan behind all external events and know his love for me can never fail. I am at peace in his perfect plan. My peace comes from deep within and is not based on my circumstances. I follow my inner wisdom.

AUGUST 28

I uproot the negative in my life at its root:

I ask for and receive God's guidance. I accept the truth about myself. Forgiveness and God's love heal me of all dis-ease in my life. Joy and serenity fills my Spirit. I have common sense and wisdom and make good choices in my life. My choices grow my Spirit and not my ego. My sanity is sound and secure and is powered by God's love for me.

AUGUST 29

I grow through adverse situations:

I choose my words carefully and do not feed comments that should not grow. I feed the positive and starve the negative. I am an encourager and not a discourager. I see mistakes as opportunities to grow. I am aware of my real motivation in the things I do. I am not motivated by ego growth but Spirit growth. I know when to say no to things of the ego. I am always able to be grateful and see God's loving hand working in my life.

AUGUST 30

My thoughts produce heaven on earth:

I am a grateful person and see good. God's creative power is behind all life, and I am part of that creative force. I rely on and acknowledge God's presence in my life and walk strongly in the power of the Holy Spirit. My mind and body are powered by the divine Spirit within me. I am a source of encouragement and divine revelation in this world. God uses me daily, and I have purpose. I rely on God's Spirit within me, and Christ lives through me. I surrender my will for God's will and rest secure in his perfect plan.

AUGUST 31

I am quick to forgive and feel no need to judge:

In Christ, I am completely forgiven, and I trust God with all judgments of this world. My mind and Spirit rest in God's divine plan, and I feel peace. I surrender my day to the Holy Spirit's leading and hear the voice of God. I have eyes to see the spiritual and ears to hear the voice for God. I respond to God willingly and grow daily in faith and wholeness.

SEPTEMBER

SEPTEMBER 1

My Spirit is controlled by God's Spirit:

I listen and obey the Spirit within me. God uses the difficulties in my life to refine me. I grow daily in God's will for my life, and his peace fills my Spirit. I am quick to forgive the errors of others and do not hold a grudge. I surrender my ego's desire to God's will. I accept the things I can't change and change the things I can. I have the power of God within me and live in his grace. God's divine purpose is being worked out in my life.

SEPTEMBER 2

God's blessings continually flow on me:

My life reflects God's presence within, and I am filled with a grateful Spirit. I am precious to God, and he desires to bless me. My conversations are pleasing to God, and they are a source of encouragement to others. I ask for and receive more of God's wisdom daily. My daily decisions are based on God's wisdom within me.

My life reflects common sense and balance impregnated with God's Spirit.

SEPTEMBER 3

I am patient, kind and humble and look for the best in all situations:

I am not easily provoked or offended and have burned up my records of wrongs. I treat others as I wish to be treated. The love of Jesus flows through me. I am able to feel God's leading in my life and respond to his voice within me. I think and act with God and know it is not my responsibility to judge the thoughts and acts of others. I do the best I can and leave the rest for God to do.

SEPTEMBER 4

I know I am not responsible for the choices others make:

I see errors as opportunities for learning. I do not condemn others for mistakes they make. I do not throw the first stone. I am the master of my thoughts and I have chosen to surrender them to the Holy Spirits guidance. Jesus is my constant companion, and he is always with me waiting for me to put every thought in his hands. I am able to eliminate unhelpful thoughts. My mind is filled with thoughts that bless and recall the truth that is within me. I reject the false for the sake of the truth.

SEPTEMBER 5

I choose my thoughts carefully:

I always choose forgiveness over condemnation. Two wrongs never make a right, and I am conscious of not adding to a wrong by my behavior. I do not strengthen false ideas. I bring love to those in pain. I think and act right. I dissolve all fear in my life with love. I remember that I am God's child as are all my brothers and sisters. I relinquish all false thoughts that separate me from God and know God's love for me. I am part of God's eternal plan and that can never change.

SEPTEMBER 6

I am aware of my thoughts:

When I feel angry or depressed or needing to defend myself, I root out the source of the guilt and/or shame that lies behind my action. I bring it to my awareness and then release it. I practice self-forgiveness for any and all guilt I feel. I do not blame others for my problems. The judge and jury lie within my own thoughts. I dissolve the guilt within me by accepting self-forgiveness and God's forgiveness. Guilt and suffering have no place in my life. I claim my wholeness in Christ.

SEPTEMBER 7

My peace and happiness is not dependent on others:

I am also not responsible for the peace and happiness of others. I release others of all grievances I hold against them. I answer the call for help from others but do not make them indebted to me or keep them bound to me beyond their will. I let others come and go gracefully in my life. I help others when I can and gratefully receive help when needed. I am grateful for the people God has placed in my life.

SEPTEMBER 8

My perception of situations is expanded, and I no longer feel attacked:

I receive correction with gratitude and adjust my course of thinking. I learn from difficult experiences and avoid future suffering. My union with God grows stronger each day, and my mind is brought in alignment with the Spirit within me. I surrender to the will of God and experience his joy and bliss in my life.

SEPTEMBER 9

I do not reject others:

I am faithful to the truth that lives within my own heart. I walk through the door of truth that God holds open for all to enter. Truth never ceases to be true, and my mind is open and willing to accept God's truth. I am not a victim of what happens to me but learn from all my experiences. I accept my experiences as blessings and not punishments. I embrace truth and reject illusion. I accept the divine mind within me and trust in its divine leading. My goal is certain to succeed.

SEPTEMBER 10

I face my fears, then place them in God's hands:

I know he walks beside me as I walk outside of fear. God's help is always greater than my biggest fear. I willingly change my mind about negative attitudes I hold. The Holy Spirit allows me to see the circumstances of my life though the loving eyes of Christ. Through the power of the Holy Spirit, I am able to love myself and others through any situation. I trust in God for the right answers to my prayers. My focus remains on the eternal *now* and not the past. My open heart embraces the changes in my life, and I see God revealed more and more. I am able to look beyond my own preconceptions.

SEPTEMBER 11

My security rests in God and not other people or large assets:

The divine love within me frees me from attachment and allows me greater intimacy and more freedom in my relationships. I do not try and control other people but look within for my own intentions. I surrender all my doubts and fears to God's loving and eternal plan. I find peace in knowing he loves me and has a divine plan for me. My life has purpose and value. I am God's own child. God's goodness rules my life, and I live in peace.

SEPTEMBER 12

I am able to see the pain and hurt behind the negative behavior of others:

I do not cause further pain but quickly forgive their actions and show love. When I am in fear, I tell the truth. I reveal all my dark thoughts to the healing power of God's light. I surrender my judgments of others to Jesus and am able to see through the eyes of Christ. I do not try and justify my anger and am able to admit it when I have made a mistake. I learn from the errors and mistakes I have made in my life and see them as blessings leading me home. I learn life's lessons and move forward in God's grace.

SEPTEMBER 13

I am here for a purpose:

As God reveals that purpose to me, I walk closer to his perfect plan for my life. I master the lessons of life set before me and make corrections in my course of action. I surrender false pride and the desire to impress others for God's wholeness in my life. I do not judge others who admit their mistakes but admit my own and release the rest to God.

SEPTEMBER 14

I take time to hear God's voice:

I listen to the Spirit within me and slow down. I consider the course my life is taking and make Spirit led changes. I take time to experience my life and not live as a victim of my life. My life is a gift from God, and I value the experiences it gives me. My life is the experience that allows me to grow into the truth of my real identity—a child of God completely loved and loveable.

SEPTEMBER 15

My worth is not determined by the external in my life:

My value is determined by God, and that can never change. I release the emotions and experiences that keep me from God's unconditional love. I am able to see God's unconditional love in my life and in everyone's life. I offer love to the wounded people around me and to my own wounds. I see myself as God sees me and have awakened to the truth of my real worth that is not dependent on anything or anyone. I am not deceived by the ego I live with but focus on God's perfect Spirit that lives within me.

SEPTEMBER 16

I do not put conditions on loving myself:

Conditions and situations don't change my worth; real love will never change, and God's love is real. I see myself through God's unconditional love for me. True happiness lies within me. God's love is firmly established in my heart and external events can never change that truth. God's love within me allows me to encourage the hurting around me. God's unconditional love can heal all who are willing to see another way. I search my heart and mind daily and surrender all to God's perfect plan. I have peace, placing my problems and presence into his divine plan. I grow in my understanding of God's unconditional love daily.

SEPTEMBER 17

I am not a victim of the physical world:

My soul has awakened to my true worth, and I am firmly rooted in God's love. I love myself and therefore am able to accept the love of others. My love for myself is not conditional, and I remember that God's love for me never changes. My life is secure in the love of God. In every situation, I give love away as my gift and encourage others to find the source of love in their lives. I encourage others but don't try to fix them. I spend time alone and use it as an opportunity to accept myself and the love that lives within me even deeper. I give up my ego for the certainty of God's unfailing love. I am Spirit-led and not ego-led. In every situation when I feel fear, I immediately turn it over to Jesus. I uproot the core issues of my fear and crucify them with my ego. I am a new creation in Christ; the old has been burned in the refining fires of my life.

SEPTEMBER 18

I am not a victim:

I do not hold grievances or attempt to punish others who abuse me. I let those who abuse me go free. I pray for them and bless them and gently release them. I willingly forgive myself and release others from my judgments. The veil of fear in me has been replaced by the love of God.

Love increases in me as I forgive myself and others. I am on my homeward path.

SEPTEMBER 19

I have no secret shame:

God's love and light dissolved all darkness and his light shines through me. Simplicity and clarity rule my life, and I have no hidden agendas. I communicate in truth and love with clarity. I confess my negative thinking and am healed. I do not hide negative thoughts but place them in God's healing presence. I accept each mistake I make as a gift that allows me to make corrections in my life. I celebrate the opportunity to clear my inner being of all manipulation and deceit. I bring the dark places in my mind to the light of conscious inspection and am healed. I do not defend my mistakes but confess them and am set free. My life is a clear channel that allows God's light and love to flow through.

SEPTEMBER 20

I am filled with common sense and trust the Spirit that lives within me:

There is no deceit in me. Confession and forgiveness are tools in my life that end suffering. I speak the truth in love to God, to myself, and to all I meet. All sin and shame are flooded out by God's loving light. The light of Christ shines through me. I know there are no mistakes that cannot be corrected and no error that cannot be forgiven. God's grace for me is all-inclusive, and there is nothing I can do to separate me from his love.

SEPTEMBER 21

God's loving presence encompasses me:

I am worthy of his love. God's love for me is unconditional, and that will never change. I am in partnership with God and a part of his new covenant. The Kingdom of God reigns in my own heart and there is no separation between us. I reclaim the eternal love communion with God. I no longer see myself alone and separate. My loving presence is needed in this world and I share God's love and gentle words with others. My answers and salvation come from God. I do not preach but merely show God's love to those around me.

SEPTEMBER 22

I do not judge others:

God's love is for everyone. I remember how loveable I am to God and accept my role in God's plan. I am reconciled with God and He empowers me to do His will. All darkness in my life has been replaced by God's all encompassing loving light. I do not place conditions on my love. I have answered God's call for love in all circumstances. I extend love and am not attached to the outcome. I know God's perfect plan is at work.

SEPTEMBER 23

I am part of God's perfect plan and worthy of His love:

I am able to interpret the words and actions of others in a loving way. I am not easily offended and don't feel victimized or abused. I know that God sees me loveable and worthy. I live in the present moment and don't project the past into this moment. I don't project past hurts and scarcity on the people and circumstance of the present moment. I am not a victim of life and I choose to see the positive around me. I am safe in God's plan and His love surrounds me. I choose thoughts that bring peace to my life. The peace within me spreads to those around me. My past is forgiven, and every moment is an opportunity to choose again.

SEPTEMBER 24

I expose my deep wounds to air and sunlight:

God makes me aware of all my hidden agendas and my unconscious pain is healed by God's love for me. I forgive those whom I believe caused me pain. God provides for my every need, and I am worthy of his loving care. I see myself through the eyes of Christ and know my worth. My wounds are healed by the love that flows through me. I am whole and free of guilt and sin as God created me. I accept my spiritual wholeness and reject the lies of the ego. I am a part of God's eternal love and that can never change.

SEPTEMBER 25

God gives me good gifts:

I am not misled by God's gifts to me but wait for him to reveal their real meaning. God's gifts do not feed my ego but are of a higher order. I am developing my true nature and purpose in partnership with the divine mind. I look beyond my fears and feelings of unworthiness to the divine spark of God that lives in me and everyone. I focus on the peace that lies within me.

SEPTEMBER 26

I have a grateful Spirit and focus on God's love for me:

I am worthy, and God meets my needs. I extend love and gratitude to every situation I encounter. I live within a circle of grace and surround myself and others with God's unconditional love. I am able to see everything in my life as a gift from God. I look beyond the world's interpretation and choose to see the love of God in all things. A choice for gratitude in all things makes me happy. I trust God's eternal plan and am not discouraged by the world's view. God's plan can never fail. I sow good thoughts today and reap the results in my future. I accept all of God's gifts with gratitude. I bless others instead of condemning them. I release the judgment I feel for others into God's loving hands and am free from the desire and need to judge others.

SEPTEMBER 27

My worthiness comes from God, and that can never change:

God's love for me is unconditional, and I extend his love to others. The grace of God covers all my fears, and his peace surrounds me. Christ is born in me, and I am free of all unworthiness, resentments, and need to attack others. I am filled with love, gratitude, and abundance.

SEPTEMBER 28

I have a patient Spirit and wait for God's will to be done:

I trust in his perfect will and timing. I am sensitive to the conditions at hand, and my words and actions are led by Spirit. I accept the conditions in my life as gifts from God. My happiness does not lie in things or people. I recognize the attachments in my life and the need to not make them the source of my happiness. My spiritual roots are deep and cannot be moved. I sway with the winds of life and meet life's storms without resistance. I enjoy being alive and dance through life in the arms of God.

SEPTEMBER 29

God's unconditional love surrounds me:

I am aware of this love right now. I draw my awareness of God's presence to me and hear the voice of God. My outward circumstances can never change my inner truth. God loves me, and I am part of his divine plan. God's divine presence leads me to my personal purpose.

I surrender to the circumstances in my life and do not judge by outward appearance. I do not find fault with myself or others but surrender the outcome to God's perfect will.

SEPTEMBER 30

I see God's loving presence in all things:

There is no place where his presence cannot be found. I am secure in his gentle, protective, and all-encompassing care. I place no limits on God, and he is beyond my definition. My essence is a result of his presence in me, and that is eternal. His steady, loving presence is drawing me back to eternal knowledge. My wisdom and understanding increases daily, and my true essence is remembered. I remember my spiritual connection to all beings. I remember God throughout the day and focus on what is totally acceptable and lovable. I dedicate my thought life to God's loving presence.

OCTOBER

OCTOBER 1

I speak encouraging words and see the spiritual behind the physical:

I affirm who I am in Christ. I do not argue about words and beliefs that separate me from others. I am able to see what we share in common and focus on the positive. I search for the truth in every situation. God made me whole and complete and from that place I celebrate and accept all those he puts in my life. I am a peacemaker wherever God places me.

OCTOBER 2

I am able to see spiritual equality:

I am not fooled by apparent circumstances that have distorted my beliefs in the past. I know that all are equal and worthy in God's plan and I accept my spiritual identity. I respect the free will of others and take responsibility for the choices I make. I practice equality by seeing beyond the physical. I remember that I am not a body only. My real reality lies in my Spirit and my connection to God.

I am not limited to the body. God's power lives through me. I let go of the conditions that reinforce my suffering and awaken to my true identity. I am the hands and feet of God's love and forgiveness in the world.

OCTOBER 3

I accept God's love for me and know that it extends to all:

I am a source of comfort to those around me and have compassion. I am able to see others through the eyes of Christ and know we are all equal in God's plan. I have eyes to see the truth and am not deceived.

OCTOBER 4

I am committed to the truth:

When necessary, I can say no in a loving way. I do not support hurtful behavior in those around me. I tell the truth but respect the free choice of others. I share my thoughts and advice when asked with honesty and humility. I am aware of appropriate boundaries. I learn from those I perceive as enemies and value the teachings they bring me. I am able to see through the eyes of my enemies and develop compassion. I do not have to agree with my enemies in order to love them. God's unconditional love flows through me.

OCTOBER 5

I perceive the Spirit of God in others:

My Spirit is able to listen to the Spirit in others, and I know our equality. I have an attitude of respect and acceptance for others. God's miracles flow from my love for others. I am always willing to give everyone a fair hearing. My love and belief in equality tolerates differences in perspectives. I have the courage to disagree and the wisdom and foresight to maintain an environment of equality. I am willing to consider the perspectives of others. I do not destroy in word or deed those I disagree with. I see the essential worth in all individual human beings. I love, respect, and learn from the opponents in my life. When appropriate, I am willing to change my mind.

OCTOBER 6

I walk on the path of compassion:

I love and accept all beings as equals. God's peace rests within me and within all my brothers and sisters. I affirm this peace in myself and others. There is no place for judgment in my life. I am part of Christ, and no judgment is valid. I treat myself and others as I treat Christ. I know that love must be deeper than agreement. The source that goes beyond judgment and fear lives within me. I trust God's plan and know that nothing I can do will cut me off from God's love for me. I choose for my awakening into all God intended me to be. I am guided by the Spirit of God and am at peace.

OCTOBER 7

My thoughts reflect good seeds:

I speak good words about others, and my words are reflected in my actions. I see myself in others and always look for the good. I remember that those who strike out at others are those who are hurting. I carefully watch my thoughts, words, and actions. I build up others and recognize their need for love and forgiveness.

OCTOBER 8

I see others as I wish to be seen—forgiven and loved by God:

I acknowledge the wounds in my life and give them to God for healing. I acknowledge all repressed pain within me and surrender it to the healing power of God. My body, mind, and spirit are filled with God's wholeness. I forgive others and accept forgiveness for myself. I offer love and hope to those around me. I accept others as I wish to be accepted and am a peacemaker. My thoughts are changed, and I am empowered by the Spirit within me. I make Spirit-led choices in what I think and say and how I act. I remember God has given me free will to be led by ego or Spirit. I choose Spirit.

OCTOBER 9

I look beyond my ego-based perspectives:

I ask for the Holy Spirit's leading in all decisions I make. I am led by Spirit and learn life's lessons. I take responsibility for the situations in my life and acknowledge the fears that cause the pain. I am undoing the false ideas and beliefs I have about myself and others. My mind is released from all false goals and ego-generated desires. I am content in the present moment and know that each present moment that lies ahead allows me a choice to be at peace. I always choose the peace of God over the strife of the world. I choose to be wholly present and attentive right now. I choose to be happy right now. I will not wallow in the past.

OCTOBER 10

I am not a victim of time:

I do not live the past in the present but treasure the precious now. I have forgiven the past, and it has no hold on me. I learn from those I would condemn and judge as guilty and forgive myself and others. I realize my wholeness cannot be compromised or damaged in the spiritual realm. My eternal self is secure in heaven. I choose to see the eternal and not the temporal things of this world. My spiritual eyes are open to the unchanging plan of God. I walk through all fear in faith and focus on God's loving plan for mankind.

OCTOBER 11

I use my thoughts to unite and not separate:

I seek out the unity in people and ideas. I do not attack other people's thoughts. I extend respect and trust for others even when I don't agree. I see what links me to others and not what separates us. God accepts me and others as we are. His plan is not derailed by our errors and differences. The open wound below my ego has been healed by Christ. I no longer defend and protect my ego as it has been replaced by the love of God. I willingly give up the limited, temporal self of the ego for the unlimited, universal Spirit living within me. I rest in God's promises.

OCTOBER 12

I place my complete trust in God and accept his complete forgiveness:

God's forgiveness follows me everywhere, and there is no place I cannot receive it. I let go of every painful thought and release it to loving forgiveness. I do not allow my thoughts to imprison me. The peace of God fills my thoughts, and I choose to see everything through the eyes of Christ. I hear the voice of God and give and accept forgiveness freely.

OCTOBER 13

I accept God's pure, unadulterated, unconditional love:

God's love for me has healed me. The love of God surrounds me. I am a reflection of God's love to the world around me. I practice unconditional love without regard for the outcome. My body and mind are whole, and God's loving presence flows through me. I accept God's love for me with grace and heartfelt gratitude. I engage in loving acts, wanting nothing in return. I see the inner beauty in others and share the light within me. I affirm to others that they are loved—in words and also wordlessly.

I accept others exactly as they are. I monitor my thoughts, words, and actions to reflect unconditional love. I do not allow others to take advantage of me but allow others to take responsibility for their life. God's perfect plan is working in everyone. God's will, will be done.

OCTOBER 14
I love without regard for what might be returned to me:

The love I give without qualification returns to me a minimum in equal measure. I accept others as they are right now. I empower others with my love and acceptance. I look past emotional scars and superficial imperfections in myself and others. I look past material existence to the spiritual essence within. I know forgiveness is always appropriate and all can and should be forgiven. I forgive myself and others every day. I forgive and then heal the wounds. I address the root cause of actions; I forgive in love and open-hearted acceptance.

OCTOBER 15
I embrace the love that lives deep within me:

Love is my past, present, and future. I was created in love by my loving heavenly Father. I am a part of his loving eternal plan. My blemished thoughts are being purified, and I am released from the errors of my past. All less than loving thoughts and deeds have been forgiven. I love without purpose and separate my desires and agendas from unconditional love. I do not reduce the purity of love by my expectations but by faith knowing it is infused with Spirit.

OCTOBER 16

I focus my love on Spirit and not on the flesh or material world:

I experience God's love in everything that surrounds me and feel deep contentment and gratitude. I am guided and supported by a loving God and trust the unfolding of my life to his perfect plan. I accept each moment of my life as God's gift to me. I check my motives when living love. My ability to be genuinely loving grows daily, and I am able to accept and give God's unconditional love.

OCTOBER 17

God's love is limitless:

I am grateful for whatever my life gives or takes away from me. I give thanks in all things and experience each day with love in my heart and light in my steps. I love myself regardless of what is going on in my life. I am able to love myself because God loves me. My value is not in what I do but in who I am—a child of God, a loved member of God's family. I accept who and what I am. I treat myself with respect. My thoughts, emotions, and actions are love-based. I recognize the light in others even as I realistically recognize their other aspects. I give thanks for whatever life brings my way. I recognize the love of God behind the events of my life and give thanks.

OCTOBER 18

I look for ways to express joy and laughter:

I am able to see humor in situations when they are not at the expense of another. Lightness and brightness surround my being. I create laughter in my life to stimulate joy and create more room for love. I use laughter and humor to lift or shift the burdens that come into my life. I do not allow the burdens of the physical world to weigh down the freedom of my spiritual being.

OCTOBER 19

The foundation of my life is God's love:

His love for me cannot be moved, interrupted, or disrupted. It will never erode, and no test can destroy it. My life is built on the firm foundation of a love that is secure. God's love transforms limitation into limitlessness, and boundaries no longer exist. It is a love that transcends all borders and barriers in the material world. I am certain of God's love for me despite the challenges of this world. I remain steadfast in the love of God.

OCTOBER 20

God's love flows through me:

God's justice is clothed in love, and I give and receive, secure in God's will being done. My errors do not derail God's plan; it is certain, and I am a part of that plan. I was created for a purpose, and God's will for me will succeed. I am in the process of becoming all he intended. I am shedding the physical for the spiritual and awakening to my wholeness in Christ. I accept my true value as a child of God. I am secure in his perfect plan.

OCTOBER 21

I give from a center of love:

My motives are pure, and I do things because I am a reflection of God's love. I show respect and worthiness for myself and others. I spread unconditional love and accept God's unconditional love. I bless others, and I am blessed. My love for others is not based on expectations. My love for others has no strings attached, and I am able to love and let go. I bring pure love to my relationships and not expectations and assumptions. I am not burdened by relationship baggage. I have released myself of the hurts and wounds of the past and am whole.

OCTOBER 22

My faith whispers words of comfort and hope:

I am able to trust in the unseen. I am able to love and forgive without hesitation or condition. I love without regard for what is returned to me. Faith allows me to have unconditional love and complete forgiveness. All that happens in my life fits into God's divine plan. I choose and control how I respond to what goes on around me. I choose faith over fear and serenity over anger. I am rooted in a faith that will endure whatever my physical life throws my way. I live in grace—God's gift to me.

OCTOBER 23

I grow daily in my understanding of God's everlasting love:

I hold steady to my faith regardless of the tests placed in my life. I turn my trials into treasures. I see beyond my immediate circumstances and am full of light, joy, and peace. My heart is open to the love that emanates from all that is. I stand in the light of the holy and am filled with the peace and joy of the divine. I am at peace regardless of my outward circumstances. I live with quiet joy and see blessings around me.

OCTOBER 24

I see God's Spirit everywhere:

My faith leads me to trust in the unseen. My faith leads me into the realms of the uncontrollable. I give unconditionally and share without expectations of personal gain. I recognize the Spirit at work in me and honor it over ego gratification. I trust in God's power at work in everything.

OCTOBER 25

The ultimate source of my security is faith:

As a child of God, I am living within the flow of the natural order, which provides for my needs. My needs are met by God and not my works. I trust God's provision for my life. I am a child of a loving and compassionate Father who knows my needs and knows my heart. My life is an open window through which the Spirit of God flows freely. I am filled with the gentle breeze of his presence.

OCTOBER 26

I believe in a loving God and know:

God exists in the unseen, and there are no limitations of what is possible. I trust that his will, will be done and do not place limitations on a limitless God. I place my trust and confidence in the unseen over the seen. I factor love, forgiveness, and faith into everything I do. I believe in the existence of a benevolent Creator, and that belief is reflected in my everyday life. The Spirit of God penetrates my physical eyes, and I see through Christ who lives within me. Christ's presence within me allows me to live a life of wholeness. I surrender all the challenges of this world into divine will and am one with Christ.

OCTOBER 27

My focus is clear:

I attend to the Spirits leading in my life. I embrace my spiritual being as well as my physical existence. I have a relationship with God, and the Spirit of God helps me with all my decisions. My purpose is to serve God. I allow my faith to pervade all areas of my life—every moment, circumstance, challenge, and commitment. It is a constant in my life, patient and steady. Faith is woven into every aspect of my life. It is my anchor during good and rough times. I do not lose my faith when faced with life's challenges. I focus on serving Spirit and not my ego. My faith grows moment by moment, and I am able to experience more and more of God's love for me and others.

OCTOBER 28

I don't allow others to be the source of disappointment in my life:

I take responsibility for my thoughts and actions and let others do the same. I ask for and receive the Spirits leading in my life and surrender the results to his perfect will. I trust the love and wisdom of God over my limited vision and keep focused on his perfect will being manifested in my life. I welcome and see the extraordinary presence of God in everything. I surrender the disappointments in my life and affirm gratitude for everything—yes everything—right now, always, and forever.

OCTOBER 29

My trust is placed in God:

My life is based on Spirit-infused decisions, and I am able to accept and receive more and more of God's grace. I stay on the course of Spirit, and my faith blossoms. I am united with God and his love for me. I am part of his perfect plan. My past does not interfere with God's will for me. I exist as a result of God's will and external plan for my life. I do not allow my ego to overtake my faith. I am relaxed in my will, having surrendered my preferred results to the Spirit. I commit this day to God's leading.

OCTOBER 30

I am able to see the truth:

I release all false perceptions of myself. I am able to see blessings where others see burdens. I set aside frustrations and judgments and the desire for more. I nurture my interior climate with peace and harmony regardless of external circumstances. I allow God's grace to flow through me, and I am filled with health and wholeness. I am an open window, allowing Spirit to flow through me.

OCTOBER 31

I replace knowing about God to knowing God:

I surrender to the will of God. I willingly give up my security-based needs. I trust in Spirit to guide my life and am led by inspiration. God is my navigator, and I can and do trust in his best for my life. I set aside my agendas for God's way and live comfortable and courageously in the moment. I access and integrate the teachings of Spirit in every decision I make. My soul is grounded in faith, and I release ego control to the light and love of the Spirit.

NOVEMBER

NOVEMBER 1

I choose to be grateful:

My love for God burns away fears and doubts and releases me from the desires and attachments of this world. I look and see God's love for me and am a grateful person. My love for God is without condition, and I grow stronger in faith and love through trials. I am becoming all that God intended. I have accepted my inheritance as his child. I possess the treasure of God's love.

NOVEMBER 2

I practice non-attachment to the material:

I spend my time, energy, and resources on eternal and spiritual treasures. I give away what I no longer need and simplify my life. I surround myself with what I truly love and release the stuff I think I should have. I am not burdened down with superficial distractions. I treasure wisdom over things, insight over objects, and love over possessions.

NOVEMBER 3

I remember my inner truth:

Faith is the foundation for my peace of mind. It sustains me when my life is calm and when it is choppy. Whatever comes my way, my inner peacefulness prevails. I know I am loved, guided, and cared for by a loving God. My external conditions can never change my inner truth. I remain strong in my faith regardless of the challenges of life.

NOVEMBER 4

I exhibit faith despite my challenges:

I always choose faith over fear and love over hate. I see the divine in everything I think, believe, do, and say. I am able to discern the messages and essential truths of Spirit. I seek Spirit-based thinking and am able to hear God's voice. My mind is open to the messages of Spirit, and I am Spirit-led. I choose to follow faith-based principles and hold firmly to my faith. I trust in the unknowable that is secure in God's love for me. I affirm my love for God in the midst of threatening situations and choose faith in his perfect plan over the fears of this world.

NOVEMBER 5

My Spirit contains the seed of love and light:

I surrender my will to faith in God. The stage setting of my life is blessed, and I see God's hand in my life. My union with God gives my life meaning, and I exist as part of his perfect plan. I am worthy of complete forgiveness. God forgives me all, immediately and comprehensively. I accept complete forgiveness so I can extend it to others. I forgive without expectation of an apology, the payment of a debt or the honoring of an agreement or compensation for a transgression. I forgive and cleanse my physical, psychological, and spiritual being of all anger and feelings of victimization festering inside me. Forgiveness makes me healthy physically, mentally, and spiritually.

NOVEMBER 6

I remember I am whole in Christ:

I do not allow others' attitudes and actions to keep me from wholeness. I forgive for the freedom it gives me. I release myself from the bondage of another's actions. I am able to maintain my integrity from a place of detachment rather than attachment. I give myself the gift of forgiveness and am able to see the best in myself and others. I live in God's grace.

NOVEMBER 7

I know my worth and am able to set proper boundaries:

I am able to feel compassion for others without taking on their pain, patterns, or priorities. I do not forfeit my own boundaries in order to relate. I am one with God and one with all his creations. I am able to see the wholeness that God created and know I am a part. I am open-hearted and egoless, and I live in the power of God's Spirit that lives within me.

NOVEMBER 8

I release my will to the will of God:

I release control over the outcome of my actions. I release the need to force one conclusion over another. I desire and submit to the will of God in every situation in my life. I trust in God's will for my life and believe in his love for me—unconditional and everlasting. God allows me to see with nonjudgmental understanding, unconditional peace, and irrevocable wisdom. I surrender to the will of God that makes all things whole according to his perfect plan. I do not need to manipulate people, situations, or things but put my trust and faith in God's will. I acknowledge my limited awareness with my physical mind and release myself from the physical and open myself to see the spiritual working in this world. I see the will of God being done in and around me.

NOVEMBER 9

My bond with God grows stronger daily:

I am blessed with insight and inspiration that allows me to be of further service to God. I am filled with God's unlimited love, grace, and peace. In prayer, I honor God, and my heart is still. I am surrounded by God's everlasting love. I focus my attention, emotions, talents, expertise, and resources on the spiritual. My actions express my beliefs. Moment to moment, I choose faith over fear. I practice peace and patience and know God's will, will be done. As a child of God, I have infinite potential and unlimited support. I am able through intention, belief, and support to give birth to new realities. I monitor my spoken assumptions and unspoken attitudes and allow Spirit to open my eyes to the unseen.

NOVEMBER 10

My heart is filled with love for God, and I am able to resist temptation:

I make good choices for my body, mind, and spirit. Through the power of Christ in me, I am able to overcome the temptations of this world. My faith derives from my ability to trust in the unknowable. My faith covers whatever occurs in my life. I affirm my love and belief in God by my words and actions. I choose faith over fear in every situation.

NOVEMBER 11

I remember God's love for me and my love for God:

I desire to be of service to God. I see myself as an enlightened servant of God. I am able to separate the face of the ego from the enlightened Spirit within me. I focus on the love and light of Christ that lives within me. God's light fills me with health and wholeness. The light within me enlightens my life, and I claim its healing power. I surrender my will to faith in God completely. I do not confuse the stage setting of my life from the truth of my reality. I claim Spirit, light and love, and my union with God. I am a part of God's perfect plan, and his will, will be done in my life.

NOVEMBER 12

I willingly accept God's total forgiveness:

I forgive others as I have been forgiven. I am released of the guilt of unforgiveness. I no longer place conditions on my love and criteria by which I forgive. God sees, loves, and forgives every part of me. The burden of unforgiveness and guilt has been lifted from me. I am whole and holy in God's sight. I honor God by forgiving others. I am a person of compassion, caring, and committed to loving others.

NOVEMBER 13

God's light surrounds me:

There are no strings attached to my forgiveness. I am cleansed from the physical, psychological, and spiritual results of anger and judgments that were festering inside me. I release the toxic memories stored within me and fill the space with the healing light of love. My biochemistry is in balance, and I am healthy and whole. I do not allow others' attitudes and actions to imprison me. I release myself from toxic relationships by always forgiving. I allow others to act with honor and integrity.

NOVEMBER 14

I choose to see God's presence in others:

I am open-hearted and nonjudgmental. I am a part of God's divine plan, and I recognize and affirm this same plan in others. Compassion replaces ego, and the

Spirit of Christ is revealed through me. I desire to let God's will live through me. It is not my wish but God's will that takes first place in my life. I release control of my actions to faith in God's perfect plan. I give up my narrow thinking and preferred conclusions to the will of God. I surrender to God's will in every situation and affirm my faith in his divine plan. I trust God's blessing, understanding, and wisdom in all the circumstances of my life. I surrender and accept my life without question, regret, or redefinition. I have faith that the will of God is being done on earth as it is in heaven.

NOVEMBER 15

I accept God's total forgiveness:

There is nothing (no thing) I have done that has not been forgiven. I accept God's forgiveness and, as a result, am able to forgive others. I do not place conditions on my love and also do not place conditions on forgiving others. God's love for me unburdens me of all guilt and unworthiness. I release myself from my self-assessments and accept God's view of me. I am totally accepted and loved. I honor God by forgiving and showing compassion, caring, and commitment to loving others.

NOVEMBER 16

I am a forgiving person:

I forgive others without expectation of apology or recompense. I let go of the desire for a specific response or behavior. I release myself and cleanse myself from the anger, judgments, and feelings of victimization that I have held within me. I release the memory of trespass and my body, mind, and spirit are perfectly balanced. Forgiveness gives me health and well-being. I always choose forgiveness over dis-ease and sickness. My healing is not dependant on others. I reject pious-self-righteousness as a reaction to wrongs against me. I reject negative emotions and hostile behavior. I do not belittle others by my words. Forgiveness releases me from unhealthy connections.

NOVEMBER 17

I see God in others with compassion and an open heart:

The Spirit of God connects me to others, and I am able to relate compassionately without being drawn into their pain and destructive patterns. I turn to the strength of Spirit within me and overcome the challenges of this world. I see the common bonds in others that draw us together and refrain from judging. I seek God's will first in all situations and release control of the outcome of my actions. I give up my preferred results to the will of God. In every situation in my life, I ask that the will of God will dominate. I trust the will of God over my limited understanding and surrender in faith those things I don't understand. I am released from the need to control what happens next. I place my faith in God's nonjudgmental understanding, unconditional peace, and irrevocable wisdom. I look beyond what I see in the physical and acknowledge the spiritual working in this world.

NOVEMBER 18

I am a servant of God:

I pray for further insight and inspiration and am able to serve God greater. I pray to be filled with the light and love of God. I rest in the peaceful pool of love and am blessed by the serene mercy of the divine. My actions and words express my spiritual beliefs. I welcome events that challenge my faith and grow stronger through them. My faith is firmly planted, and I am able to see the possible beyond what the world deems impossible. My thoughts are Spirit-based and are not limited. I have infinite potential and unlimited support from Christ who lives within me. I focus on God and his intentions and will and am able to see beyond the natural. I work with God to transform possibilities.

NOVEMBER 19

I hear the voice of Spirit and obey:

I focus my attention, emotions, and time on the eternal. I emotionally tie myself to God's truths and not the lies of the world. What I purport to believe and my words and actions do not vary. I believe in God's perfect plan and don't rebel at the tests that strengthen my belief. I can overcome whatever comes my way and am secure in God's loving care for me. I realize the power of my unspoken attitudes and thoughts. I reject those that do not align up with God's plan. I make good choices, and

God's blessings fall on me. I am a thankful person because I come from a loving God.

NOVEMBER 20

My heart is filled with love for God:

I am not tempted by bad choices or any choice that leads me away from Spirit. Faith flows freely through me, and I share it freely with others. The emptiness of the past is filled with the fullness of faith. I am firmly embedded in God's love and lack for nothing. The spiritual vessel that I am has no cracks. I do not allow life's circumstances to create cracks and drain me of faith. Every opposition, setback, and situation turns me to my faith, and I grow stronger. I am energized and inspired as I face challenges. The fullness of Spirit keeps me grounded, and the winds of life do not sweep me away. The fullness of faith within me fills me with hope each day. I delight in God's eternal plan for my life.

NOVEMBER 21

I seek the grace of God:

God's plan gives me extended periods of grace. My attitudes are based on God's truths, and I am at peace. My faith cushions the bumps in life, and I weather the ride, secure in my faith. Love is reflected more and more in the choices I make, and I am able to see through the eyes of Christ. I am being guided, comforted, and led by God's Spirit within me.

NOVEMBER 22

I claim the state of grace given me:

I accept my true identity as God's child and his creation. I experience God's Spirit more and more and hear the voice of God. I am Spirit-led and am able to see beyond the obvious. I flow with the forces of nature and Spirit in my life. I am secure in the choices and directions the Spirit leads me to take. I am led by the divine hand of the Spirit. I am infused with the Spirit and recognize the divine within me. I breathe in the blessings of grace with every breath.

NOVEMBER 23

God's grace is showered down upon me:

I rest in the peaceful assurance of God's love for me. God smiles down on me, and I am filled with love and joy. I am cojoined with God's love in my spirit and live in a state of grace. I am elevated above the material reality but gracefully integrated with it. I live with confidence and purpose surrounded with God's love. God's presence surrounds everything I do. I accept God's grace and blessings into my life.

NOVEMBER 24

I experience the divine, and my faith is strengthened:

I see the unseen God through the eyes of grace. I embody love and light and realize my immortality as a child of God. My light is reflected on all I meet, and I light a darkened world. I am accessing the infinite potential of my spiritual presence. I celebrate who I am as an enlightened spirit in human form. My inner shining light is a beacon in the storms of life. I am light and love. I act from the love and selfless self within me. I accept my spiritual nature and am grateful my steps are surrounded by the light of God's love. I am never alone.

NOVEMBER 25

God's wisdom flows through me:

I have eyes to see God's glory, patience to wait for his will, and diligence to continually seek to know him better. My heart is dedicated to God, and my life proclaims his presence. I am blessed, and the peace of God surrounds me.

NOVEMBER 26

The foundation of my life is firmly planted in the Spirit:

I am able to see God in all that is, and I experience God's presence in my life. I affirm his mighty presence and power within me. I speak the truth in love and plant good seeds in others. I release all darkness in my life and am filled with the light of goodness. I uproot darkness at its source. I grow stronger spiritually through overcoming the darkness that comes into my life.

NOVEMBER 27

I embrace the light of God, and darkness is dissipated:

Each choice I make affirms the light within me. I affirm the Spirit of God living within me and affirm it to others even when they don't acknowledge its presence. I steadfastly reflect light even when darkness surrounds me. I use unconditional love as the antidote to darkness. The light within me is greater than any darkness in this world. My life is light-infused.

NOVEMBER 28

I forgive instead of blame:

I show love in every situation, refrain from judging, and avoid fear and anger. God's gifts are hidden within me. God's ultimate plan will be accomplished within the framework of my free will. My Spirit is being reborn into knowing the source of the perpetual Spirit and light that anchors my being. Difficulties lead me to Spirit and the light and love within me, which is God. I face my greatest fears, and God is there. I move into the unknown, knowing God will never leave me. I am loved and guided by a love that never ends.

NOVEMBER 29

Today I begin anew:

I am in the process of healing, completing, and balancing my past actions. I choose to make better choices in the present and redeem the failures of the past. God forgives all, and I align my actions and thoughts with his total forgiveness. Each moment is a new beginning to live from the Spirit within me—to choose goodness and God's way. I am guided by the love and light that lives within me.

NOVEMBER 30

I maintain inner peace amidst turbulence:

I do not allow turbulent situations to affect my tranquil peace, which is centered in God. My body, mind, and spirit are aligned with God's wisdom and light, and I act from a place of power and peace. The tranquility within me allows me to think with clarity. In every turbulent situation, I focus on God's tranquility that is my strength.

DECEMBER

DECEMBER 1
Throughout the day, I remember that:

Darkness can never conquer light. I engage in the conflicts of life by being light. I never use darkness to fight darkness. I claim my spiritual dimension and react to darkness with love, light, and commitment. I am strong and serene. I see uncertainty as a gift and not a curse. I look for the jewels in the upheavals of life. I appreciate what I have and create space for fresh perspectives. I let go of what is gone and look forward to what is to come.

DECEMBER 2
I recognize the power of my mind:

I feed my mind adequately and am able to consider situations with balance, clarity, and integrity. I am able to see beyond the darkness of this world and claim love and light over fear and darkness. The spiritual power within me overcomes the world, and I choose mastery over misery. My mind is filled with love and gratefulness. I acknowledge the grace of God that surrounds me and know that I am loved. My mind is filled with positive thoughts, and I am supportive of myself and others in the thoughts I have and the words I speak. My days flow with the natural rhythms that surround me and I am Spirit-led.

DECEMBER 3
I replace all fear with faith:

I believe in a positive outcome to my life. I counter fear with adequacy, competence, and worthiness as a child of God. I face fear with faith and learn from its lessons. My Spirit becomes stronger as I choose to remember that I am God's child—loved and protected. I rest in God's loving hands regardless of my circumstances in this world. My focus is on the eternal and not the temporal. I am at peace.

DECEMBER 4
God's love surrounds all my actions today:

I am able to speak the truth without judging. I am quick to forgive and slow to anger. My body is cleansed of all toxic anger, and the Spirit is not hindered. The Spirit within eliminates all limitations and frees me to be all God created. Limitation is replaced with love. I am not afraid to face the unknown. God surrounds me with his love.

DECEMBER 5
Christ speaks through me:

I act and speak without denouncing others. My words and deeds are simple based on my own truth. I release all fear and insecurity into God's divine plan and am at peace with his perfect plan and love for me. I am a person of integrity. I tell the truth and stick to the facts. I do not compromise the internal sense of who I am as God's child. I do not give up myself to fit into groups. I am true to myself and my innermost beliefs.

DECEMBER 6
I am authentic in word and deed:

I do not balance the negativity I perceive by negative responses. I never choose revenge over forgiveness, hate over love, or divisiveness over unity. I feed the light and love in this world and not the darkness. Instead of punishing, I work to heal, empower, and release bondage and despair. I offer hope in every situation. I affirm the value and beauty within everyone and encourage them to honor the Spirit that lives within them.

DECEMBER 7
My mind is clear:

I am able to make clear-headed assessment of the people and circumstances that surround me. I look for the spark of Spirit even in the darkest encounters. I practice self-perpetuating optimism in every situation

I encounter. I choose to see God's perfect plan being woven behind the tattered frayed ends.

DECEMBER 8

I recognize the Spirit within me:

I never sacrifice Spirit for social acceptance. I am not tempted by those things that diminish the light and love in my life. Temptation gives me an opportunity to reaffirm the Spirit within me. I make good choices in the words I use, in the foods I eat, in the things I buy, and in the people I associate with—I increase the light in my life. I make conscious choices that please the Spirit within me.

DECEMBER 9

I am able to see the bigger picture:

I choose the greater good over selfish interests. I make choices that build up the Spirit within me. I find win-win solutions to the discord around me. I always aim to create harmony and accord and encourage growth amidst dissent and discord. I am centered in the peace that dwells within me. I am led by Spirit and rest in God's perfect plan.

DECEMBER 10

I look for ways to simplify my life:

I practice simplicity in my life. I do not complicate my life with more goods than I need or use. I do not keep or acquire more of what I do not need. I am not driven by ego-based materialism. I keep my life simple and leave plenty of space and time to be filled with Spirit. I am filled by Spirit and not stuff. I make good choices in the things I purchase and the way I spend my time. I do not burden myself with useless stuff and aimless events.

DECEMBER 11

I use my time wisely:

I energize myself with proper food, sleep, and relaxation. I am efficient with my time; my thinking is razor-sharp, and I am a creative person. I am slow to anger and am optimistic and hopeful. I am open to love in my life and share it generously. I take time to renew my physical and spiritual strength and am rewarded with energy and effectiveness.

DECEMBER 12

I accomplish the goals set before me:

I am not a procrastinator. My self-confidence comes from who I am in Christ. I do not find reasons to delay actions I need to take. I handle the things I need to do and cross them off my list. I am capable of handling the things I need to do and let go of the "shoulds" that have no real value. I discern the important from the unimportant and do not waste my time. I am not a procrastinator.

DECEMBER 13

I am a positive influence on others:

I encourage others to grow and strengthen their capabilities. I am not required to recognize or acknowledge the self-assigned superiority of another. I have no need to challenge their opinions or deal with their arrogance. I refuse to participate in the dynamics of arrogance and affirm my own value and capabilities. I refrain from judging messages and actions that are birthed in arrogance and remind myself that arrogance results from feelings of superiority and vulnerability.

DECEMBER 14

My mind and life are not filled with the useless:

I keep and maintain those things and feelings that enrich the Spirit within me. I have no need to accumulate and surround myself with more and more stuff. I am not a hoarder of time, things, and emotions. I allow Spirit to flow through me freely and am not burdened by useless baggage. I release the things I don't need, rid myself of harmful emotions, and am released from the need to hoard others time. I place my future and faith in God's loving provision for my life and believe in his abundance to meet my needs.

DECEMBER 15
God created my value, and because he did:

I value myself. I am God's child, and I remember my inheritance. I do not and will not sell my spirit for security in this world. I do not bargain away part of myself and allow darkness to replace the light within me. I make choices that increase the light of Christ within me. I am Spirit-led.

DECEMBER 16
Today:

I honor the Spirit within every situation, and my spirit is strengthened. My loyalty or disloyalty is based on spiritual growth. I am loyal to the Spirit and disloyal to whatever compromises it. I base my actions on love, forgiveness, and the good of all more than self-interest. I bring light to darkness. The Spirit within me surrounds me, and I am secure. I am complete in Christ and rest secure in my spiritual home.

DECEMBER 17
I invite Spirit into all my activities:

I find joy in my work that honors me and others. I am constantly learning, growing, and creating in new ways. My life is Spirit filled. I am energized and lead a balanced life able to do those things that further connect me to the Spirit within. I am empowered to do God's will.

DECEMBER 18

I am becoming all that God intended:

I am a person of integrity and compassion. I act with love in all situations and refrain from judging. I live in the light from moment to moment and do not base results in the material realm. I am faith-filled and secure and accept what is. My actions are covered in love, and I detach myself from the outcome. I have faith in my Spirit-led actions and believe in God's appropriate conclusion. I act with integrity and pure intentions and leave the results to God. I make decisions that strengthen Spirit within me.

DECEMBER 19

I notice my memories today:

I face the issues in my life with truth and honesty. I learn from my memories but do not live in the past. My memories do not create barriers in the present, and I do not carry the limitations of the past into the present. I treasure the Spirit-filled memories of the past, and they uplift me in the present.

DECEMBER 20

I give thanks for God's divine plan:

I focus on God's love and light in my life. I acknowledge the present, knowing God is in all things. His divine plan exists behind all the dramas of this life. I focus on God's plan and not man's. My positive thoughts counter all negativity in my life.

DECEMBER 21
I claim the inner strength that lives within me:

God's power within me makes me psychologically and emotionally strong and healthy. I invest time and energy to keep my equilibrium regardless of the actions of others. The thoughtlessness of others is given to Spirit for interpretation. I am a forgiving person and show compassion. My wounds are healed by the light and love of God, and all negativity is released from my body. The inner strength within me is my shield and safety. I am centered on Christ within me.

DECEMBER 22
Regardless of what happens today:

I act with integrity in all situations and treat others with respect. I speak the truth and honor my values. My energy is directed toward positive purposes. I am guided by Spirit and embody wholeness. I look for goodness in the people and circumstances around me. I remain steadfast in my convictions and true to my core.

DECEMBER 23
I live in the present:

I do not waste my energy and attention on regret. I can trust myself to make good decisions in the present and rely on Spirit to direct my thoughts. I learn from the past and avoid repeating negative actions. I act with Spirit in every situation. I am growing into oneness with God and appreciate the lessons that bring me closer to my destination.

DECEMBER 24

God's light and love surround me:

I honor my Spirit in solitude. I grow daily in heartfelt compassion. The choices I make are birthed in the intention to be love and spread light. My words and actions exemplify the Christ within me. I am constantly aware of the formless Spirit that lies within me. I look beyond the matter of this world and recognize God's Spirit. I honor the Spirit within me and all creation and see and experience light and love. God is beyond form and the formless contains no darkness. I am light.

DECEMBER 25

In every situation today, I choose carefully:

I always choose the Spirit over darkness of form. I acknowledge ultimate reality as formless and focus on the love and the light that is my Spirit. I focus on the light that is pure Spirit within me and experience light, love, and peace. I am able to see myself as God created me, and it is good.

DECEMBER 26

I acknowledge the Spirit within me:

I am filled with Spirit and therefore filled with light. There is no place for darkness within me. I am blessed beyond measure. I learn the lessons of my lifetime and make more Spirit-based choices. I have and am progressing through the darkness of the past and encompass Spirit in all areas of my life. I face darkness that enters my life and remove it by the power of Spirit. My wounds have been healed, and I move forward in light and love. I make choices that bring me closer to God and strengthen the light and love in and around me.

DECEMBER 27
My words reflect hope:

I act on the hope that is within me. I claim the Spirit's leading in all the circumstances I encounter. Where there is Spirit, there is hope. I choose to think positively about situations in my life and take the necessary steps toward positive results. I maintain positive thought patterns and attitudes about potentialities in my life. I fuel my faith by acknowledging that Spirit exists in all situations. My behavior actualizes my faith in Spirit. I envision and expect God's light to radiate from all my actions. I know that love exists everywhere because God is everywhere.

DECEMBER 28
My actions are a reflection of my hope:

I act from the center of God's love and have hope. I accept God's love and light within me all the time. Spirit guides my actions and takes me through each trial of my life. My declaration of hope is supported by my actions, and I affirm that there is always reason for hope. I reaffirm the Spirit by the hope within me. My actions bring me closer to God.

DECEMBER 29

My actions today lead me closer to God's will:

I think positively about a situation and take steps to make it so. I have a hand in constructing most of the circumstances that surround me. I recognize that my inaction can influence as much as my action. I nurture hope in all situations by affirming that Spirit exists in all situations. I act and behave as if hope were an observable part of my reality and not just an idol wish. Light radiates from my existence and is obvious to everyone around me. I remember always that love exists everywhere because God is everywhere.

DECEMBER 30

I search for the positive in every situation and know:

My higher purpose is clothed in love and light all the time. I focus on the higher purpose of my life. I allow the Spirit to energize and guide me through both victories and perceived defeats. The Spirit provides me with the wings of hope. I am a person of faith and action, intention and attention, and prayer and pragmatism. I am a vessel and vehicle for God's love and work. I have the ability to look beyond the immediate situations in my life and focus on the positive. I focus on the working of Spirit in my life, and my words and actions reflect an optimistic outcome. I consciously choose to be optimistic regardless of the worldview. I am an optimistic person.

DECEMBER 31

I walk in confidence knowing that:

God gives me confidence in his divine path for me. I am equipped to do the work he sets before me. My confidence is surrounded by competence, insight, fortitude, and grace. My life is touched by the Spirit, and I acknowledge it leading in every areas of my life. I hear the voice of Spirit and following its leading. I am able to see the miracles of life around me. I am aware of its presence in everyone and everything. My mind and heart are open to the power of Spirit, and I am a grateful person. I use my mind and Spirit, conscious and unconscious thoughts, intentions and actions to accept the miracles of God into my life.